Eve Arnold

TO MY BELOVED GRANDCHILDREN
DAVID, MICHAEL AND SARAH
(IN ALPHABETICAL ORDER)
WHO ARE ALWAYS READY FOR
A CUDDLE, A HUG AND LAUGHTER.
WITH LOVE.

First published in Great Britain 2002
Editions des Cahiers du Cinéma for the Original edition 2001

Bloomsbury Publishing Plc, 38 Soho Square, London W1D 3HB

A CIP catalogue record is available from the British Library

ISBN 0 7475 5917 1

10 9 8 7 6 5 4 3 2 1

Art Direction Paul Raymond Cohen
Printed by Artegrafica S.p.A. Verona, Italy

Eve Arnold

FILM JOURNAL

CONTENTS

John Huston plans a shot for *Under the Volcano*. With him are Gabriel Figueroa, the great
Mexican lighting cameraman, his operator and Jacqueline Bisset, the female lead.
Mexico, 1983.

INTRODUCTION

Over a period of fifty years I have photographed movie stars on location and off – at the studio and at home, at work and at play, when they were filming and when they were between films. Beginning in the fifties, a new genre of photography emerged in which a film company engaged a professional photographer to tell a story of the making of the feature in pictures and words. This kind of document was to be totally different from the usual studio portraits done by the studio's own photographers, who dealt in fantasies. People like Hurrell would glamorize the stars, flatter them with careful lighting, dramatic posing and retouching. These studio photographers dealt in dreams. The photojournalist on the other hand dealt in reality, using whatever light might be available, not posing, not retouching, but letting the personality and the situation come through. This kind of picture reporting was not new – it goes back to the beginning of photographic time; it was its application to films that was new. Its purpose was to produce a photo essay of high professional standard which was to prove invaluable in promoting the film when it was released.

I find among my serious documentary photographs a body of still photos and text I made on forty films, mainly in the fifties and sixties when Hollywood was still glamorous but, as Jill Robinson, Dore Schary's daughter, puts it, 'in the last scenes of its third act'.

Eve Arnold watches Joan Crawford make up for *The Best of Everything*. Photo: Gordon Parks. Hollywood, 1959.

My real work begins with Marlene Dietrich in 1952, then Joan Crawford's last major film, *The Best of Everything*, made in 1959, and ends with Joe Losey's last film, *Steaming*, made in 1984. In between were five John Huston films, among them *The Misfits*, *The Bible* and *The Man Who Would Be King*. There were films starring Clark Gable, Marilyn Monroe, Richard Burton, Simone Signoret, Sophia Loren, Vanessa Redgrave, Orson Welles, Laurence Olivier, Paul Scofield, Marlon Brando and Isabella Rossellini, to drop a few names. There were also slews of animals: the ones in Noah's Ark in *The Bible* and the ones in *Doctor Dolittle*.

Over the years I learned that the stills photographer is often allowed great intimacy with the star. The daily contact on the film set encourages trust to be built between the person being photographed and the photographer. This makes for a chance to show aspects of the star's personality that would otherwise be almost impossible to portray. If the chemistry is right between star and photographer and if the geometry of the pictures pleases the star, often the two people end up with a long-term professional friendship during which they continue to work together and to produce highly personal images. Such was my case with John Huston, Vanessa Redgrave, Marilyn Monroe, Isabella Rossellini and Mikhail Baryshnikov.

I also learned that the photographer must retain personal integrity and tell the truth at all times, being careful not to become a hired flack for the film company. It is as though the camera has no ears, so over the years I became privy to much that was personal and private: Joan Crawford stripped and insisted upon being photographed in the nude. Marlene Dietrich talked about making

Eve Arnold on the set of *Becket*. Photo: Robert Penn. England, 1963.

love with President Kennedy. Clark Gable glowed when he talked about being an expectant father at sixty-three. Simone Signoret talked about her husband (Yves Montand)'s infidelities. Isabella Rossellini talked about her mother (Ingrid Bergman)'s affair with the photographer Robert Capa. Charlie Chaplin talked about ageing and was most curious about the sex lives of the Georgian centenarians I had photographed. James Cagney sang dirty Yiddish ditties that he had learned growing up on the streets of New York. Marilyn Monroe brushed her pubic hair while being interviewed for a magazine article.

Please note, in order to try to give a broad-based and varied understanding of the work of the photojournalist I have included notes, quotes and some excerpts from my published books. Text to go with pictures was usually written on the same day the pictures were made, in an effort to keep the immediacy of the instant impression. The dates given in the book are when the pictures were taken, not when the films were released.

In addition to the forty-some films I documented, I also photographed innumerable picture stories and single pictures (that might have taken from an hour to months to complete) when the movie people were between films. To give a fuller picture I present a few examples:

Marlene Dietrich, Gloria Swanson, Paul Newman, James & Willy Cagney, Silvana Mangano, Gina Lollobrigida, Shirley MacLaine, Danny Kaye, Alan Bates, Dirk Bogarde, Ingrid Bergman, Martin Ransohoff, Jean Shrimpton, Michelangelo Antonioni, Vanessa Redgrave, Audrey Hepburn, Joe Losey, Irene Papas, Kim Novak.

MARLENE DIETRICH

(1952)

The first movie personality I photographed in depth was Marlene Dietrich. It was lucky for me, because she was a consummate professional. I learned a lot from that session and reaped the benefits of having it published first in *Esquire* in the USA and then worldwide. That single story acted as a launch pad for me to personality and star photography.

Late one rainy night I received a call from Columbia Records to cover a recording session of Marlene Dietrich in which she would sing the songs she had sung to the Allied troops during the war: 'Lili Marlene', 'Miss Otis Regrets' and others. Marlene was my first 'personality', and I was thrilled.

I had heard that when she recorded she dressed in trousers and a beret, but on the evening we worked she arrived in a short cocktail dress on which there was a large gaudy diamond clip. The other get-up would have been more appropriate, but there were the wonderful legs instead. She was trailed by two men. One was Jean Gabin and the other a short, pock-marked man whom she introduced as a friend from Hollywood. Adroit questioning revealed that he was her astrologer and that he had decreed that this miserable wet night was the propitious time to make the recordings. The time was certainly propitious for me. She worked diligently –

Marlene Dietrich singing songs she made famous during World War II, at a recording session.
New York, 1952.

'like a ditchdigger', said my notes – from midnight when she arrived until six in the morning. I followed her from rehearsal to recording to playback and back again as she worked, and nothing was questioned or off-limits. I heard later from our mutual friend Leo Lerman that she called him when we finished and complained that I had been there all night taking pictures. He asked why she hadn't stopped me. She said it had never occurred to her, I had done it with 'such authority'.

Magnum, the cooperative photo agency that represented me, had been informed by Columbia Records that either I could have twenty-five dollars, with the negatives belonging to them, or I could receive no payment and own the negatives. Of course I chose the latter. There was also a stipulation that Marlene would have to vet the pictures and have final right of approval. And she wanted to see them immediately. I went straight from the session to my darkroom (an improvised cupboard that had formerly housed a large refrigerator in my bedroom and which I had to enter sideways because it was so small). I printed carefully to make her look as young and attractive as possible.

While I worked, there were phone calls from Columbia Records to arrange a time next day for me to see Miss Dietrich with the pictures. There was also a call for me to meet Madame Edmonde Charles-Roux, then editor of French *Vogue*, to show her my portfolio. I arranged to go to *Vogue* first, and from there to Marlene. Madame C. loved my portfolio, she said, but what was the second envelope I was carrying? Could she see it? Another time, I said. But what was it? Embarrassed, gauche, I told the truth: Marlene, I said, but she insists on seeing the pictures first. Nonsense, said Charles-

Roux: just let me see them – I'll never tell Marlene I saw them. Too inexperienced to deal with the situation, I showed her the pictures. Again she reassured me that she would say nothing.

I went directly from *Vogue* to Marlene's house, where there was a message to say that she was away for the day and for me to leave the pictures and my phone number. That night the *Vogue* editor went to a party given by Condé Nast for Marlene and told her she had seen terrific pictures of her done by me. Marlene's fury was predictable. She called the record company and raged. I had broken a sacred trust. She was to have seen the pictures first. How dare I? She said she had been so angry that she had torn up the pictures without looking at them. The PR person from Columbia Records called me. What to do? I had another set of prints made by a commercial printer and sent them to Miss Dietrich.

When she went through the pictures she wrote instructions on each (in eyebrow pencil) for retouching: narrow down the chin, cut down the waist, remove the dimple from the knee, the ankle should be slimmer, etc. I went into the darkroom again, printed them well, wrote captions and a short text and took the pictures to *Esquire* magazine, which used them across two pages. I did not retouch them – just printed them well, and removed two prints she might have found offensive.

The picture story was to be reproduced in many magazines around the world and to be a forerunner of the changes taking place in portraiture – a documentation, a form Alexei Brodovitch, the legendary teacher and *Harper's Bazaar* art director, called a 'portrait in action', unglamorized and unretouched. When he saw these pictures Bob Capa said my work fell, metaphorically of course, between Marlene Dietrich's legs and the bitter lives of migratory potato pickers. (He was right. My work still continues with the celebrated and the poverty-stricken.)

Marlene loved those pictures, and for years I was her 'white-haired girl' (I went grey early) and was brought in on many occasions, from her opening the circus to an appearance at the Museum of Modern Art and more recording sessions.

It was flattering to be invited to photograph Dietrich, who knew a great deal about photography. She knew exactly how she should be photographed to bring out the exquisite line of her cheekbones, the luminosity of her eyes, the arch of her neck, the beauty of her legs. When she was in Hollywood she would discuss with the cameraman where her key light should be, the angle of the fill light, etc. A story that went the rounds was that she was particularly pleased with the cameraman after *Rancho Notorious* (Fritz Lang, 1952) was filmed and offered, as a reward, to go to bed with him. When he demurred she laughed and sent him a Cadillac instead.

Recording sessions were stimulating to photograph, because everything was in motion: the subject, the musicians, the technicians and therefore the photographer. You needed fast reflexes to keep up with moving targets, and sensitivity and skill to get the pictures while keeping out of the performers' eyeline so as not to break their concentration. You also needed to be careful not to photograph during soft musical passages so the click wasn't heard on the recording. Even now when I think about it I feel the tension in my muscles that I felt then while waiting for fortissimo passages in the music.

Photographing recording sessions was particularly difficult because at the time I was still using the square-format Rollei, an awkward camera to compose in. Pictures seem to design best in rectangles because the eye sees that way. Filling the square space (at least at first) takes longer to arrange and one always worries that with a fast-moving subject, pictures are being missed: that you're just a beat behind. But the Rollei was the camera of choice in the fifties. Historically, it bridged the period from the even larger studio-format camera to the smaller and more flexible 35mm camera.

I fell out of favour with Marlene in the early sixties. She did a show at the Olympia in Paris and, hearing from a friend that I was in Paris, got in touch with me. She had demanded that *Match*, which was doing a feature on her, guarantee her a cover. It was during the time of the Algerian crisis, and plastic bombs were exploding all over Paris. When the magazine pointed out that under the circumstances it might need the space for a more compelling situation, she asked me to photograph as well, so she could threaten *Match* with the competition of other French magazines. When I saw the pictures I made, I knew she would hate them. It was almost a decade since the first session, and to paraphrase an old Hollywood joke, the photographer was ten years older. I decided to retire them, and sent her a note saying that I had lost my touch, had done a bad job, and was so sorry; I had tried to reach her to tell her myself, but had been unable to. Then I left for London on an assignment. Stupidly, I left the pictures at Magnum in Paris with strict instructions for them to be locked away and not be used, but she was clever – she came to the office herself and with a combination of charm and intimidation managed to see the

pictures. She was imperious and pitying: 'Sad,' she said, 'but poor Eve has really lost her touch.'

At some point in the sixties when I was photographing Marlene in Paris, she talked about President Kennedy at a dinner party. She said she had been invited to Washington to address a group of Jewish war veterans. When she arrived in Washington there were two limousines waiting for her. One was from the White House, so she took that one. She was driven to a special door in the back of the White House, all the time uncertain of who had sent for her and wondering how anyone knew her whereabouts.

She was then ushered into a lovely suite of rooms where an attractive negligee awaited her. She played the game, put on the negligee and then Jack Kennedy joined her. She said she was concerned for the protocol as to how to proceed as well as the fact that the President suffered from a bad back. So she didn't know which way to turn, but he put her at ease – and it was fine. When it was over and she was about to get up to go to the Jewish war veterans, he asked for 'Just one more, Marlene'. No thank you, she was already late. Then with his hand on the doorknob he turned to her, and this is what it was all about.

'Marlene, did you ever make it with Dad?'

But she said her clothes had been whisked away and freshly pressed, and she went off to her engagement humming to herself.

What had she hummed? I asked.

'"Miss Otis Regrets",' she said.

Gloria Swanson in the play *Twentieth Century* at rehearsal. Broadway, 1951.

Paul Newman in white T-shirt taking a class at The Actors Studio. New York, 1955.

James Cagney and his wife Willy hoofing in his barn. Martha's Vineyard, 1958.

Silvana Mangano becomes part of the sculpture at the Museum of Modern Art. New York, 1956.

29

Joan Crawford admires herself in her dressing room during filming of *The Best of Everything*.
Hollywood, 1959.

THE BEST OF EVERYTHING

(1959)
Joan Crawford
Director: Jean Negulesco

The first time I met Joan Crawford she took off her clothes, stood in front of me nude and insisted I photograph her. The situation was the following: I was assigned by the *Woman's Home Companion*, an American magazine, to publicize *Autumn Leaves*, a film in which Miss Crawford plays the part of an ageing woman. It was a pure publicity puffball of a scenario that a Hollywood publicist had dreamed up. I was to do an essay in pictures and words.

The idea was that Miss Crawford was concerned about the education of her adopted daughter. She was faced with a dilemma: should Christina, who wanted to be an actress like Mommie, plan to go to college in California and take up drama there while going on with her education, or should she come to New York to try to take a direct path to an acting career?

Since Miss Crawford knew no one in New York who could help, I mapped out a plan of action. We would go to theatre and supper afterwards at Sardi's every night for a week. This would give Joan maximum coverage to be seen, and it would also (theoretically) give Christina a chance to see real theatre and give her a more concrete idea of her chosen métier. During the days there would be talking to people in the theatre who might be helpful: drama-school heads, producers, directors and a young actress, Susan Strasberg, currently starring in *The Diary of Anne Frank*.

Let me describe our first day's outings. We met at Tina Leser, the dress designer's, where Miss Crawford and her daughter were to buy clothes. Joan swept in, her square-shouldered suit and very high-heeled clear plastic shoes making her appear tall (she was in reality only five foot four). On her shirt cuffs were the tiniest of dogs – one pissing poodle on each. If she put her hands together there was a muff. As she handed the dogs (Mommie's darlings) to her secretary, she kissed each on the mouth, then kissed me on the mouth (we had never met before). She then proceeded to the dressing room, where an entire wardrobe awaited her. She ignored the fact that Christina had not arrived and started to strip. When she was completely nude, she imperiously told me to start photographing. It was obvious that she had been drinking, and it was also obvious that there was something that impelled her to behave the way she did, something I only dimly began to understand years later when I had learned more about her.

At any rate, there she was nude – but, sadly, something happens to flesh after fifty. I knew she would not be happy with the pictures she kept insisting I take. I tried playing for time. Shouldn't we wait for Christina? No, we should not, emphatically not. So, I picked up the camera and started to photograph. By the time I had finished a roll of thirty-six exposures, Christina arrived. I breathed more easily. Joan put on her undergarments, Christina took off her outer clothes, they both started to put on the lovely Leser clothes, and I began to take pictures.

Late in the afternoon I staggered out of the dressing room.

I had been a fool to let her terrorize me into taking the nudes, and – bad news – I had exposed them on colour film; I had been too nervous to notice that I had colour film in the camera in anticipation of the colourful frocks I expected her to pirouette in. I realized there was no one I could trust to process the film; the risk was too great that it would be copied and exploited. Then what? I would have to process it myself, and I had never processed a roll of colour film. I raced to the nearest camera shop and bought a manual on basic colour development and the necessary chemicals, and asked for a short course from the clerk who served me.

I hurried home, mixed up the chemicals, and dressed for the evening's revels. In our party at *The Diary of Anne Frank* were the Crawford ladies; Joan's husband, Al Steele, chairman of the board of Pepsi-Cola; two young actors whose names escape me; and a man built like a Quonset hut who was Steele's chauffeur and drinking buddy. It was his job to find out which was the best bar nearest the theatre, and to set up the drinks so that at intermission, Mr Steele and his guests could get straight to their tipples.

Of course, Joan made a last-minute entrance for the first act, but by the beginning of the second act she was fortified by her favourite 140-proof vodka (a good choice – vodka has no odour). Just before the curtain was raised she made her slow dramatic entrance down the aisle, then paused, turned, and stood at her seat blowing kisses at the audience. The curtain had to be held for ten minutes while she took her bows. I should have photographed this spectacle, but the play was so serious and disturbing that it would have been sacrilege to have raised the camera at that moment. At dinner at Sardi's later, Joan said she had done it just for me and she hoped I appreciated it. I gulped and said nothing.

The entrance into Sardi's was a triumphal procession. People craned

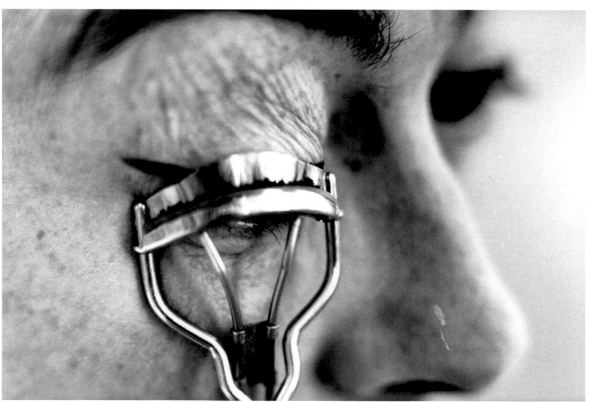

Joan Crawford makes up for a scene in *The Best of Everything* from top ...

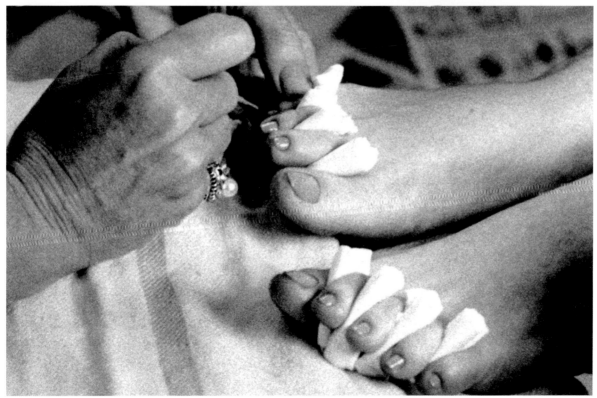

... to toe. Hollywood, 1959.

their necks, applauded, asked for autographs. Joan seated us all, ordered our meals without asking us what we wanted, and then, without apparent cause, started to berate Christina, accusing her of behaving like a harlot. I made a few token shots, excused myself and rushed home to process the roll of colour film. Intuition told me that when my subject sobered in the morning she might demand the roll of film. Hallelujah, the chemicals brought forth images – not great technically or photographically, but still passable; a weapon with which to placate my adversary.

Next morning, early, I called the Columbia Pictures publicist whose job it was to deal with Joan and the story we were involved in. I told her that Miss Crawford might call her to say that during the dress session I might have taken some questionable pictures. Well, they were now processed by me, no one else had seen them – and they were ready for her. All she needed to do was ask and they were hers.

Berenice, the publicist, was mystified but said OK when I told her it would be breaking trust to tell her more. Fifteen minutes later she was back on the phone. Yes, Miss Crawford had phoned – how had I known she would call? Laughter from my end.

The saga continued for the rest of the week, and Joan did not ask for the questionable transparencies that were ready in my camera bag. The day after the photography was finished, she phoned me herself. Command performance: lunch at '21'. This time I made the late entrance. She was waiting for me, hand outstretched – I put the little yellow box of transparencies into it. One by one she held up the transparencies to the light. She sighed, leaned across the table,

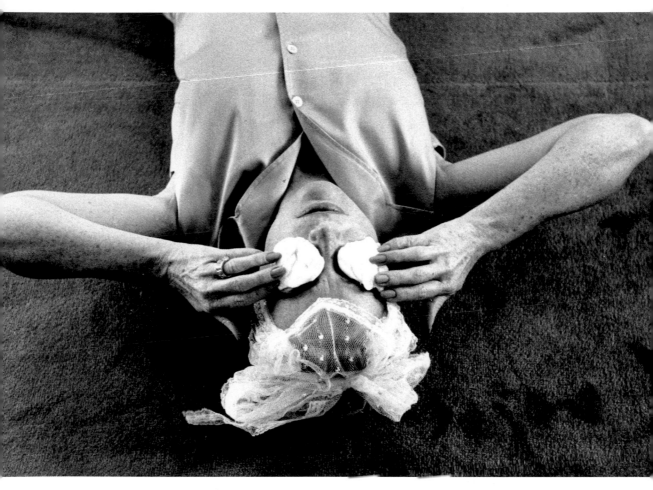

Joan Crawford rests between scenes for *The Best of Everything*. Hollywood, 1959.

kissed me, raised her vodka glass and said, 'Love and eternal trust – always.'

I had reason to remind her of this toast three years later when at my suggestion *Life* magazine assigned me a photo essay on her. She was working on a film called *The Best of Everything*, she was recently widowed, she had four adopted children, she was still echt-Hollywood, and she was on the board of Pepsi-Cola, a mix that should yield interesting pictures.

From New York I called her at Pepsi-Cola, and within half an hour she was back on the phone to me from California. Yes, she would love to be in *Life*; yes, she would love to be photographed by me; but there was one small favour – she would like to go into the darkroom with me the way Marilyn Monroe had with Richard Avedon. Translated, this meant that she wanted editorial control, and this I felt neither the magazine nor I should permit. I said I would ask the magazine and that we would get back to her.

At eight o'clock next morning, Ed Thompson, a harassed managing editor of *Life*, phoned. During the night his employer, Henry Luce, the publisher of *Life*, had had a wild call from Miss Crawford complaining that that Arnold woman was trying to withhold her (Crawford's) editorial right to say which pictures were to be used. The editor thought we should agree to her terms so Mr Luce could get his sleep. I suggested we drop the story, then played a hunch that we wait until twelve o'clock New York time on the chance that in the sober light of day she might back down. At eight o'clock her time, she called me. I reminded her that she had trusted me once before; perhaps she should again. 'Yes,' came her dulcet tones, 'I agree,' and, still in that sweet voice, 'but if I don't like what you

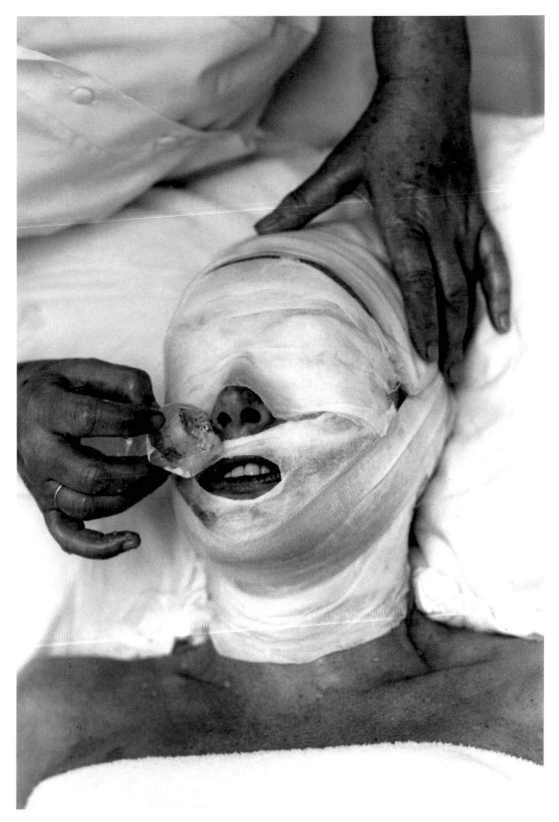

A beautician from Elizabeth Arden gives Joan Crawford a facial. New York, 1959.

do,' and here Mrs Steele's steely voice came through, 'you'll never work in Hollywood again.'

It was not the best way to start an assignment, but when I arrived in Hollywood she was welcoming. We discussed the story line – she wanted to show her fans how dedicated she had been to hang on to the top of the cliff of success for thirty years. We started off with nothing off-limits and wound up after eight weeks the same way.

In fact, so inventive was Joan (she would simply dream up situations and go ahead, waiting for the camera to follow after) that we could have filled an encyclopaedia instead of the twelve pages at our disposal.

The research about her was revealing. Joan had adopted her four children during the Hollywood days when it was easy to do so. She was between husbands, and the little blond heads beside her own in the current *Screen Gems* or other movie magazines made perfect copy for her. She is said to have stopped the show when she attended the wedding of a former lover with all four of them being ushered into the church with her.

My notes about her early history were interesting too. She grew up as a prostitute in her mother's establishment; she started her film career doing pornographic films. She spent the next ten years of her professional life as an actress trying to buy back the ever-proliferating blue movies, but they eluded her. Where there was a positive, someone would make a negative and from that negative a positive – all in a never-ending chain. In Germany someone said they are still on sale, but I have never seen one. In California a director said he was present when she and a brand-new husband had a dinner party. For entertainment the groom had ordered some

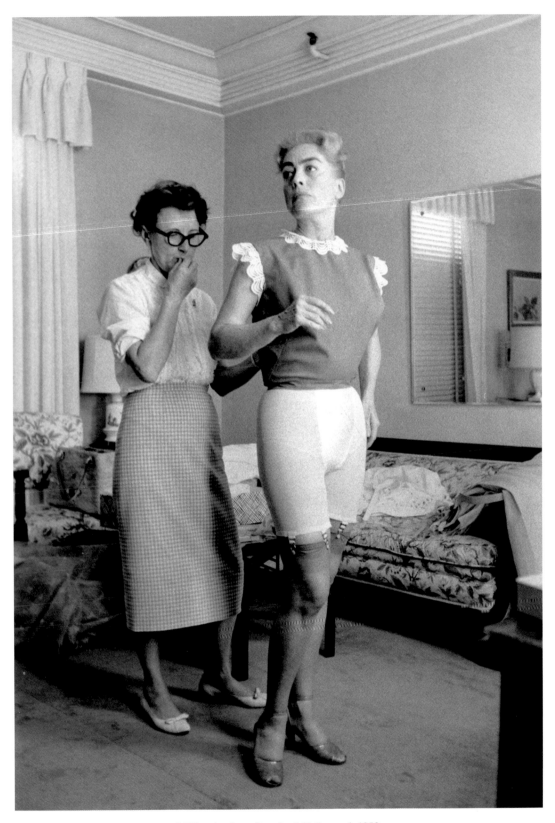

A fitting for Joan Crawford. Hollywood, 1959.

Joan Crawford trying to remember her lines during a rehearsal at home in California.
Behind her is Joan as she was in *Mildred Pierce*. Hollywood, 1959.

blue films, and one of them turned out to star his bride. True or
not I do not know. But she was the stuff legends are built around.
She was the last of the queen bees. She would arrive at the 20th
Century-Fox studio lot in her limousine. Her chauffeur would
follow her in, carrying a large thermos box marked 'Pepsi-Cola' (in
which, packed in ice, was her 140-proof vodka) and a smaller
elegant black alligator case in which were her jewels. She insisted
upon wearing real gems in the film, the idea being that their
authenticity gave her a greater sense of authority (about authority:
she kept repeating that she had 'balls'). Her precious gems were in
matched sets like costume jewellery: necklace, two clips, a pair of
earrings, two bracelets, two black pearl rings, emeralds, topazes,
rubies, aquamarines or whatever precious gems. As clasps on a pair
of diamond bracelets there were priceless baguette diamonds – one
from the engagement ring given her by Douglas Fairbanks Jr, and
the other given her by the actor Franchot Tone.

It was remarkable to see her on the set made up and ready for a
scene, surrounded by her retinue of hairdresser, make-up artist,
wardrobe mistress, secretary, chauffeur and stand-in. They would
line up beside the Pepsi-Cola dispenser Joan kept outside her
dressing room. She would stand nervously clutching her fingers and
repeating her lines to herself. For big emotional moments the
director would arrange for her to literally run into a scene. She
would take off twenty feet from the lighted set, run, hit her mark
perfectly and start to emote for the camera.

Every other day or so, her twelve-year-old twins, Kathy and Cindy,
would be brought to the set all dressed up – ruffled, beribboned and
awkward. They would sit, legs crossed at the ankles, in the shadows,

Joan Crawford and her daughter Christina, who later wrote *Mommie Dearest*. New York, 1956.

drinking Pepsi-Cola and waiting for Mommie to summon them. When she did, all that could be heard from them was a litany of 'Yes, Mommie, yes, Mommie'.

Weekends we would spend at her house in Bel-Air photographing. Those would be her days for having her nails done, her hair coloured, her legs waxed, her eyebrows dyed; all of which she wanted me to record on film, to show her devotion to her public. In the mornings she would come down the stairs slowly, pause midway at the niche in the stairwell where the spotlighted Oscar she had won for *Mildred Pierce* was housed, genuflect and continue to the bottom. Only then could the day's work begin.

The more I saw of her, the more complex she seemed and the more perplexed I became. Hollywood is a parochial town where everyone knows everyone else's business. When word got around that I was doing a *Life* story on her, people got in touch with me to tell me Joan Crawford stories – everybody from clapper boys to executives. Mostly they were stories that had to do with the children and her cruelty to them.

Joan was fond of telling about her days – her heydays – when she was at Warners. She talked about Bette Davis at Warners but would end up by saying that she, Joan, had been the 'baby of the lot', implying that Miss Davis was much older. Actually, Joan saw Miss Davis as her formidable rival. When the *Life* story appeared, she cabled me and again said, 'Love and eternal trust always.' It was a tough, intimate story, but she had wanted it that way.

When next I heard from her it was perhaps a year later and she wanted me to come and work on her next film, *What Ever Happened to Baby Jane?* She said she would be starring with Miss Davis and that I should be able to do some wonderful things. They hadn't been together since Joan had been 'the baby' on the Warners lot. I had to decline. I was living in England, my son was in school there, and I didn't want to leave him. About three months later, Joan called in the middle of the night. She was ecstatic. The film was finished. She said, 'You would have been so proud of me. I was a lady, not like that cunt Bette Davis.'

Joan Crawford with her twin daughters Kathy and Cindy and her poodles. Hollywood, 1959.

A workout for Joan and Christina Crawford. New York, 1956.

Joan Crawford reads her fan mail. New York, 1959.

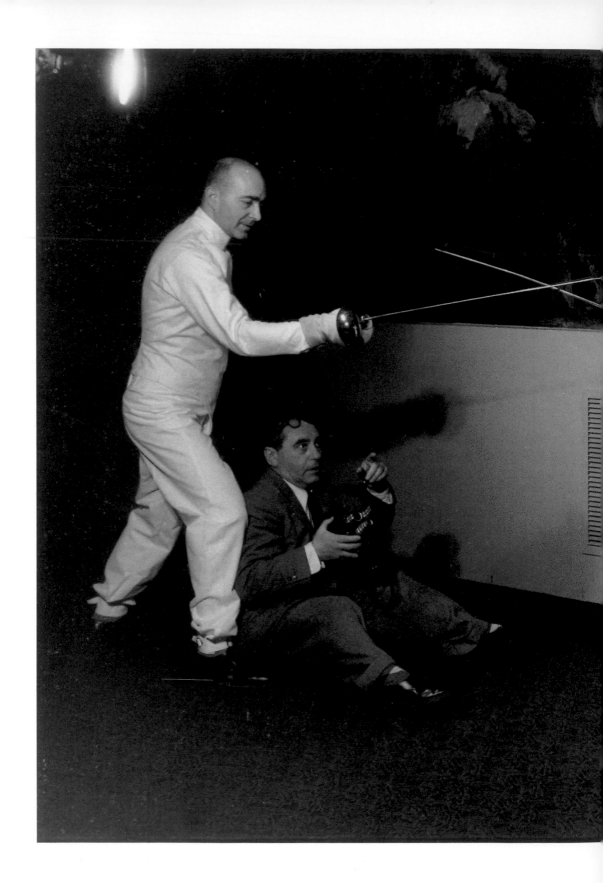

Gina Lollobrigida promotes a film in which she plays a duellist. Note photographer in the shadows.
New York, 1958.

THE MISFITS

(1960)
Marilyn Monroe, Clark Gable, Eli Wallach,
Montgomery Clift
Director: John Huston

Marilyn Monroe, another Hollywood legend whom I photographed, runs like a thread during my early work in America. We met when we were young women, each just beginning her career. She was a starlet, I a neophyte photographer. Neither of us knew very much about her chosen métier, but this formed a bond between us.

It was at a party given for John Huston that we met. When we were introduced by another photographer, Sam Shaw, who had shown her my published story of Marlene Dietrich singing the songs she made famous during World War II, she said, 'If you could do that well with Marlene, can you *imagine* what you can do with me?'

I was reminded of that mad day in 1956 when I photographed Joan Crawford in the nude, that she had talked venomously about Marilyn, whom she had just seen at the Actors Studio. She said, 'She didn't wear a girdle – her ass was hanging out. She is a disgrace to the industry'

Some weeks later when I ran into Marilyn, she told me that she had seen Miss Crawford at the Actors Studio. She was breathless with awe, stage-struck at meeting the movie star whom she had aspired to emulate when she was a child living in an orphanage in Hollywood.

Marilyn Monroe on the set of *The Misfits.* Nevada, 1960.

It is interesting to compare the two women. Crawford was of
an earlier era, of the high Hollywood time when the studio
controlled the lives of the actors – both professional and personal.
All news filtered through publicists. It seemed virtual bondage.
The behaviour of the actors was expected to be above reproach.
Their press and therefore their livelihood depended upon it.
Crawford slavishly believed her publicity. That was her identity.
Marilyn's time in film was looser. The studios were beginning to
lose their grip on the actors. The independent film-makers were
beginning to take hold. That meant that a maverick like Marilyn
could fight the studio for what she believed were her rights. Unlike
Crawford she did not believe or trust her own publicity. Watching
her during the decade I knew her, I came to believe that when she
was dreaming that she could become a movie star, she could cope
with her life, but when the fantasy became the reality she couldn't
handle it.

My professional friendship with Marilyn was helpful to us both.
She adored posing for the still camera, and her way of getting to
stardom – and staying there – was to remain in the public eye.
What better way than a picture story, which filled more column
inches than text possibly could? Remember that this was still a peak
time for the picture magazine – pre-television – the late forties and
the early fifties.

For me she was a joy to photograph, and as her fame increased she
became a source of many magazine pages, and having access to her
earned me a certain cachet in editors' eyes.

By the time we did the first pictures, she had checked out the fact
that I was a member of the prestigious photographers' cooperative

Magnum Photos, which had offices in New York and Paris and agents who distributed our work worldwide. Because I owned copyright, a story done for an American magazine like *Esquire* or *Life* also meant distribution abroad. She loved the idea of one photography session yielding multiple venues.

Our quid pro quo relationship based on mutual advantage developed into a friendship. The bond between us was photography. She liked my pictures and was canny enough to realize that they were a fresh approach for presenting her – a looser, more intimate look than the posed studio portraits she was used to in Hollywood.

I never knew anyone who even came close to Marilyn in natural ability to use both photographer and still camera. Because we were both inexperienced and didn't know what shouldn't be done, we improvised and made things work. Over the years I found myself in the privileged position of photographing someone who had not merely a gift for the still camera, as I had first thought, but a genius for it. Philippe Halsman said of her, 'I saw an amazing phenomenon of Hollywood being outsmarted by a girl whom it itself characterized as a dumb blonde.'

In 1960 Lee Jones, Magnum's New York bureau chief, approached Frank Taylor, the producer of *The Misfits*, to act as exclusive agency to photograph the film Arthur Miller had written for his wife Marilyn Monroe. No one but Magnum photographers were to be on location to record the making of the film, and we were to feed the world's press. We were to come out two by two to the Nevada location. Every two weeks there was a change of photographers, and by the time I came out the whole company seemed demoralized and Marilyn felt she couldn't continue to relate to two new photographers every two weeks. So I, whom she knew, was asked to stay on for the remaining eight weeks it took to finish the film, winding up with a studio session to shoot colour covers of Marilyn to go with the stories we had all shot.

Often the action off camera was more interesting than on camera. The entire company was billeted at the Mapes Hotel in Reno, where the gambling went on non-stop night and day. Relationships between local women and the crew developed rapidly and when the company pulled out there were tears: two bar girls were pregnant. This against the daily drama of Marilyn's sleeping-pill problems, her rift with Arthur Miller, whom she was just about to divorce, and her tardiness made for unease and worry because the film was late, over budget and was generally becoming difficult to keep on target.

Through all of this Mr Huston kept his Olympian cool. He would leave the hotel at six every morning except Sunday for the sixty-mile ride to the location, even though he might have gambled the night away, looking elegant in a pressed blue jean suit and red neckerchief. He would return when the light started to fail. Sundays were special, reserved for catching up on sleep and picnicking. Gladys Hill, who was co-author on many of his films, and who when he was shooting was secretary, assistant and general factotum, would arrange the champagne luncheon. We would take off into the desert or the mountains in a convoy of cars.

On one such junket we went to an Indian Reservation, where the tribal chieftain showed us around. He paused at the entrance to an

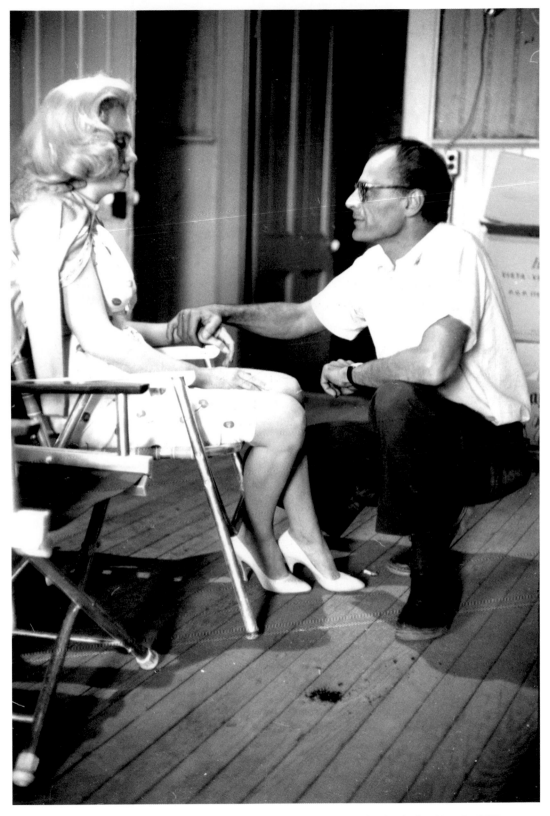

Arthur Miller and his (then) wife Marilyn. He wrote *The Misfits* as a valentine for her. Nevada, 1960.

Arthur Miller gives advice on a shot to Marilyn Monroe, while Clark Gable talks to John Huston (off camera). Nevada, 1960.

John Huston discusses sound with Marilyn Monroe, Clark Gable and sound man (backs to camera). Nevada, 1960.

abandoned silver mine and told the following tale:

At the turn of the century, a group of businessmen from the East had set up a mining consortium and had tried to get the Indians to mine the silver ore. The tribesmen were appalled at the idea, since they felt that in the process the white man would destroy a sacred mountain. When they objected strenuously, they were kidnapped and forced to work under threat by twelve supervisors who were heavily armed. Their women and children were held hostage.

The men bided their time; then one Saturday night when their captors had retired in a drunken stupor, the Indians managed to disarm them and crucify all twelve.

The chief looked slyly at Huston (whom he had nicknamed Long John Silver), shook his head and said, 'The white man only crucified one man and built a world religion around it. Can you imagine what we could have built with twelve?'

Ernst Haas, my Magnum colleague who was photographing the wild horses featured in the film, described the atmosphere that surrounded *The Misfits*:

'All the people who were on the film were misfits – Marilyn, Montgomery Clift, John Huston, all a little connected to catastrophe, Gable not saying much, just himself being Gable. It showed how some stars are like stars in heaven that are burned out. The light is still travelling, but the star is gone. They were the actors playing out the allegory, then seeing it in life. It was like being at your own funeral.'

Perhaps a bit drastic, but many days had a sense of loss, of failure, of decay.

Luckily for me, John Huston loved photographers and particularly the Magnum lot. He had been a great friend of Bob Capa's, who had initiated the idea of Magnum as a cooperative. He was wonderful to me. When we worked on the camera car he would make sure I was settled in a position from which I could get the best shots, then he would climb on.

The set always seemed booby-trapped with hazards. I had figured out a modus vivendi from the time I worked on the Crawford film so as not to become a nuisance: I learned to avoid standing in front of lights, tripping over cables, getting into camera range – especially when wide-angled lenses are being used – tripping the camera shutter when sound is running, casting shadows and especially getting into the actors' eyeline.

The least disruptive way of working was behind the scenes off camera: during make-up, hair, wardrobe sessions, in the trailer, at mealtimes. This method worked especially well with Clark Gable, who at first resisted my camera but then decided I could photograph him. One day when I had been to see the rushes I heard a voice I thought belonged to one of the grips with whom I had been making bad jokes, ask me what I thought of Clark's performance. I replied that it was great, that it knocked me on my ass. There was a great guffaw, then Clark patted me on the shoulder. When he stopped laughing, he said to me, 'You deserve some help. Come to my trailer this afternoon.' From then on he would dream up situations for me to shoot.

On every film there seemed always to be two dramas being enacted: the film itself and a parallel one behind the scenes, with the latter often being the more interesting of the two. During the days, Clark, Eli Wallach and Montgomery Clift roped the wild horses and Clark

Arthur Miller in a thoughtful mood. His marriage to Marilyn is about to end. Nevada, 1960.

Clark Gable steps into the shadows. Nevada, 1960.

had his wild emotive scenes in the desert with Marilyn when she finds out the horses are to be slaughtered for dog meat. Suddenly word flew through the unit that Clark was 'pregnant'. He was sixty-three years old and this would be his first child.

We found out when his wife, Kay, came to lunch one day. In the back of her station wagon was a cradle she had bought in an antique shop. The news electrified the entire equipe. I photographed Clark telling Marilyn; she was tender and sweet with him. (She had had an ectopic pregnancy during which she had miscarried a couple of years before.)

Clark then told me as well, but said he was sorry the news was out because he had wanted Hedda Hopper and Louella Parsons to break the news in their separate newspaper columns. However, he said he would handle it: he got Hedda to announce the upcoming birth and Louella to be godmother at the christening. Publicity as applied to films was still powerful in Hollywood.

In the middle of the night I received a call from New York. *Life* magazine had received a call from the paid informer on the unit to say 'Clark was pregnant' and would I take a picture of the empty cradle with Clark? I thought it a nasty idea and refused. There followed veiled threats of my never working for *Life* again. I stood firm. Finally *Life* called Clark – again in the middle of the night – to ask him to pose for my camera with the empty cradle. He was furious and refused. The editor at *Life* said he wouldn't have bothered Clark but they had already asked me and I had refused. To me, Clark said, 'Those jerks, what awful pictures they would have made! It's almost as though I would be standing after the birth looking at an empty cradle – too horrible a thought!' But he was full of praise for me and when the film was finished he invited me home with him to photograph him and his wife (something he never normally did). He even suggested I come back to do the first baby pictures after the birth. Alas, his premonitions were terrible to think of and I did not go back after his son John was born. I was haunted by the image of the empty cradle.

It seemed as though Gable could guard against all sorts of things. He showed me the wardrobe he had had organized for the film: gloves, chaps, heavy socks, all sorts of protective gear so that when he was pulled by the wild horses in the desert he would not be sand- or wind-burned. But he couldn't protect himself against death. Mine were to be the last photos ever taken of him and became his obituary, for he died two weeks later.

When we had finished working in Nevada, we went on to California to do some process shooting and Marilyn agreed to a studio session in Hollywood. I arranged to use the film company's (United Artists) studio and their lighting man. The producer sent a case of champagne and a kilo of caviar, and I arranged for flowers and Sinatra records.

Whenever we had worked before, it had been haphazard, more or less uncontrolled. But here we had a chance to do whatever we wanted. Marilyn had brought her secretary, her publicist, her hairdresser, wardrobe person, driver and her longtime make-up man, 'Whitey'. When Whitey had laid down the first coat of make-up, she looked around the studio at all the preparations made for her pleasure and said, 'Whitey, remember our first photo session? There was just you and me – but we had hope then.'

Marilyn Monroe rehearsing lines for her big dramatic scene (with Clark Gable) in which she hears that the wild horses are to be killed for dog meat. Nevada, 1960.

Clark Gable in an action shot, running to catch a wild horse. Nevada, 1960.

Left to right: Montgomery Clift, Clark Gable and Eli Wallach lasso a wild horse. Nevada, 1960.

Filming had begun in the Nevada desert in the blistering heat of
July and ended still in the desert in the sandstorms of November.
In spite of the chaos and difficulties endured, there was a sense of
sadness and nostalgia when the film was finished.

When we returned to New York I saw Marilyn every day for a
week while she and I went through the hundreds of pictures the
Magnum photographers had made of her. During this week she had
an interview with a European editor and she asked me to stay while
she was interviewed. When she opened the door for the woman,
she was wearing a black diaphanous robe with nothing underneath
and she had a hairbrush in her hand. While the woman was getting
her tape recorder ready, Marilyn asked whether she minded if she
brushed her hair. No, of course not, said the woman.

When she looked up, Marilyn was brushing her pubic hair.

Montgomery Clift and Marilyn go over their lines in their minds before their big scene. Nevada, 1960.

Marilyn Monroe being readied for a studio shot on the film lot. Hollywood, 1960.

Shirley MacLaine during an interview with a neophyte reporter (who forgot to turn on her tape recorder – a fact that infuriated Shirley when she found out after the interview). New York, 1960.

THE PALACE

(1962)
Documentary on Grace Kelly
Director: Bill Fry

The next film I worked on was for television. It starred Grace Kelly, her husband Prince Rainier and their two children. It was intended to show Grace Kelly playing hostess on a tour of the palace and the principality of Monaco, it was an imitation of Jackie Kennedy showing the White House.

It was interesting to go from a major film like *The Misfits* with a major director, major stars and lavish Hollywood money to a TV film where the pennies are watched and time was of the essence because time costs money. The whole operation was put in perspective when one of the crew remarked that more money had been spent on wardrobe for the White House film than was spent on the entire palace film.

It was an entirely different experience. It was November, off season in Monaco, bleak and rather triste. The casino was filled mainly by 'widows on fixed incomes' who waited each month for their assigned cheques so they could have a fling at the casino. The management at the casino had struck a deal with the 'widows'. In order to keep the tables occupied, the casino gave the women each five pounds a night so they could play off-season. During season, the women paid the casino five pounds a night to get in. So there they were these women, all dressed up and part of the props for the film.

Princess Grace and Prince Rainier of Monaco at a football match. Monaco, 1962.

Looking back I realize how unhappy we all were. The Princess seemed imperious and impervious to the crew, barely tolerating us. It was particularly difficult for me because, although she cooperated with me, it was done without grace (no gag intended). I found out why only after the picture was finished. Like many stars, the Princess had a favourite photographer, a *Life* staffer, whom she had requested. When the company insisted upon assigning me, she simply froze me out. The chill was palpable.

I did not often encounter such resistance. Usually the star wants to look good, knows how cruel the camera can be and plays up to the photographer so all is cosy. Ms Kelly was beyond this. Besides, one had the feeling that there was trouble in paradise by the way the Prince and Princess treated each other. I remember one revealing moment. One day when we were filming the pair in the palace, Her Highness in a wifely gesture started picking lint off her husband's blazer. In scarcely concealed rage he turned on her and mouthed, 'Leave me alone.'

It was an unhappy film to work on and it punctured my ego – but I learned, in a way, how to work with moody actors.

Danny Kaye conducting Rimsky-Korsakov's *The Flight of the Bumblebee* with a fly swatter. Tanglewood, Massachusetts, 1961.

Richard Burton and Elizabeth Taylor at the local pub in Shepperton where he is starring in the role of Becket. Note Elizabeth's packet of sausages that will be cooked for her dinner by the chef in her four-star hotel. England, 1963.

BECKET

(1963)
Richard Burton, Peter O'Toole,
a cameo part for Elizabeth Taylor
Director: Peter Glenville

Never could I have imagined that sunny day in 1949 when I took my first camera (a gift from a boyfriend who was a mad keen amateur photographer) down to the New York waterfront and took my first ever snap, of a Bowery bum sleeping off his excesses, that I would wind up photographing Hollywood greats. That I would lunch with Clark Gable at his home, exchange confidences with Simone Signoret, gamble with Marilyn Monroe, become a frequent house guest at John Huston's Irish retreat St Clarens, banter with Richard Burton and count among my friends Misha Baryshnikov and Isabella Rossellini.

So, here I was in England fourteen years later working on my first film assignment abroad – terrified at the prospect of photographing Peter O'Toole and Richard Burton, and wondering if I'd get a glimpse of Burton's wife Elizabeth Taylor.

As it happened, I saw a lot of Elizabeth Taylor. She would come frequently to the location outside London with Burton, we would go to the local pub after work. Although she was not supposed to be in the film, she wound up doing a cameo part.

I didn't know it at the time but there was something different about the production of *Becket*. Normally the film producer does his work back in California at the studio, but in this case Hal Wallis, a veteran producer, was with us the whole time.

Elizabeth Taylor and her children watch from the shadows the murder scene in which Becket (Richard Burton) is murdered. England, 1963.

Becket was a religious film about the murder of a priest in Canterbury Cathedral. With the big boss around all the time watching, it felt as though we were all pupils under surveillance in a Sunday school.

Pretty soon I found out why we were being watched. The two stars were drinking, and would come back after lunch word perfect but slightly tipsy. You could feel the tension throughout the studio and also Wallis's repressed anger.

In spite of the barbed atmosphere I was learning to feel easier in my skin when I worked with principal actors and I was enjoying working in England. What better place to make an historic British film than in Britain itself, where foreign film companies could tap into authentic locations, use a pool of great professional actors, have available to them functioning studios and all kinds of technical skills and aids? Also the British government had set up a financial incentive system to tempt movie companies to come to Britain to film. Add to this the comfort (for Americans) of working in a country where people spoke English – maybe, as the Americans thought, 'funny English', but English none the less.

Peter O'Toole resting during dress rehearsal for an improvised charity benefit for indigent actors. London, 1963.

Siân Phillips carries her husband, Peter O'Toole, in to triumphal acclaim at the opening party for *Hamlet*.
London, 1963.

Anne Bancroft clutching a hot-water bottle on the freezing soundstage of *The Pumpkin Eater* on the miserable Monday after John Kennedy's assassination. England, 1963.

THE PUMPKIN EATER

(1963)
Anne Bancroft, Peter Finch
Director: Jack Clayton

The Pumpkin Eater is a film ahead of its time. There were scenes
of domestic violence before the idea of battered wives became a
popular subject in the press. The film also took a different approach
to battering: the wife fights back. The fight scenes between Peter
Finch and Anne Bancroft are memorable. In them, Bancroft is
ferocious: 'She claws, hits, scratches, throws crockery, kicks and
screams with awesome reality,' said one review. Peter Finch, her
adversary, said, immediately after the scene was filmed, that he was
cowed by her performance: 'I had to remind myself she was only
acting. Thank Heaven she was only acting. I thought she was going
to kill me. My wife will never believe these bruises.'
The camerawork to shoot the scene was interesting. The camera
operator was put in a breeches buoy (canvas sling) hung from the
ceiling, and the lighting cameraman had a long stick with which
he kept moving the breeches buoy around in a circle, which gave
added movement to the fight.
I particularly remember the climate that surrounded the movie.
It was grey November and we were shooting on the Monday after
President Kennedy's assassination. The studio was subdued – people
gathered in clusters, talked in whispers. To add to my gloom and
sense of horror was the fact that I was to begin by shooting Anne
Bancroft, who I had been told hated the stills camera and didn't
much like photographers.

Anne Bancroft and Peter Finch in a knockdown marital fight. She was wild. Shepperton, England, 1963.

On the morning I saw Miss Bancroft for the first time, she was sitting on the sound stage, which was the size and temperature of a skating rink. She was covered in layers of clothing and a blanket, and was hugging a hot-water bottle to her chest.

I didn't want to break her mood but nodded to her, indicated the camera and took a shot. She indicated back that it was OK, so I kept shooting while she clutched her hot-water bottle. She was more than cooperative – in fact, a joy to photograph.

Weeks later when I got to know her, I asked how she had felt about my moving in without a by-your-leave. She said I looked so small and so lost and carrying such a small camera that she thought I didn't know what I was doing, so she kept clutching the hot-water bottle to help me out.

I invited her home for Sunday lunch to show her what I had done so far. When I projected a colour shot of her, she gasped – I feared in horror. But no. 'I am beautiful.' 'Surely,' I said, 'you must have known that?' 'No, no, no, I always thought I was ugly.' It was a joy to watch her enjoy her own good looks.

After the fight was over. Top row, left to right: the script lady, the female lead Anne Bancroft (hors de combat), the cameraman Ossie Morris. Front row: the director Jack Clayton, and the exhausted male lead, Peter Finch. Shepperton, England, 1963.

Kim Novak with her producer, one of the Mirisch brothers. Hollywood, 1964.

Alan Bates on his first trip to New York (with *The Caretaker*). Here photographed for *Vogue*. 1964.

From left to right: Gerard Malanga, Philip Fagan, Carol Koshinskie and Mario Montez. *Harlot*, New York, 1964

HARLOT

(1964)
Mario Montez, Gerard Malanga, Philip Fagan,
Carol Koshinskie
Director: Andy Warhol

In the fifties I met Andy Warhol when he was a shoe illustrator (and brilliant at it) for *Harper's Bazaar*. A mutual friend introduced us and Andy, shy, seemingly timid, pursued me pretty hard to photograph him. Even then he had dreams of glory and talked of wanting to be a star recognized by the 'smart world' out there. He was hungry for publicity. I must admit I was turned off by his attitude and surprised when he started achieving what he so baldly sought.

I didn't see him again until 1964 when I was on assignment in New York for the *Sunday Times* (London). By then he had become a leader in the art scene. I ran into him at a party and he asked me again to photograph him. I agreed to join him the following day when he would be acting as cameraman for one of his films – for the first time.

When I arrived he was standing on an orange crate in the middle of his Silver Factory with his dyed silver wig waving above the eyepiece on the camera. He appealed to the various acolytes, actors and assembled guests, 'What do I do now?'

I walked over to the camera. 'For openers,' I said, 'you push the power switch on the camera.' He did, and started to direct *Harlot*, a film with a transvestite as star, while two poets with sound equipment walked among the thirty or so people in the studio, making up the script as they went along. When they got to me, the words they came up with were, 'Who's the bird in bare feet that's taking all the pictures?' Answer, 'A friend of Andy's, but I don't think she knows what she's doing.' 'Why did she take her shoes off?' 'To feel more grounded,' I replied. And so the ad hoc, ad lib continued and was eventually used unedited.

In his films Warhol did not edit. They relate to our tolerance for seeing. By not editing he makes the viewer aware of the filming process. The results are flaws which flash past, and these are the dramatics of the film. Movies generally represent the passage of time falsely; with Warhol, time is as it is in life. His films show inaction as more eloquent than action. In this respect, it is necessary for the audience to pay close attention and contribute a great deal to the viewing. As in his paintings, Warhol asks the viewer to slow down his tempo and take notice of the seemingly unimportant details that make up our daily lives. These, isolated and minutely observed, assume enormously important proportions.

Andy Warhol with his first sophisticated anchored camera (which he operated).
The Silver Factory, New York, 1964.

Dirk Bogarde with his house guest, Ingrid Bergman, at his home in the country. England, 1964.

Dirk Bogarde with his pets in the country. England, 1964.

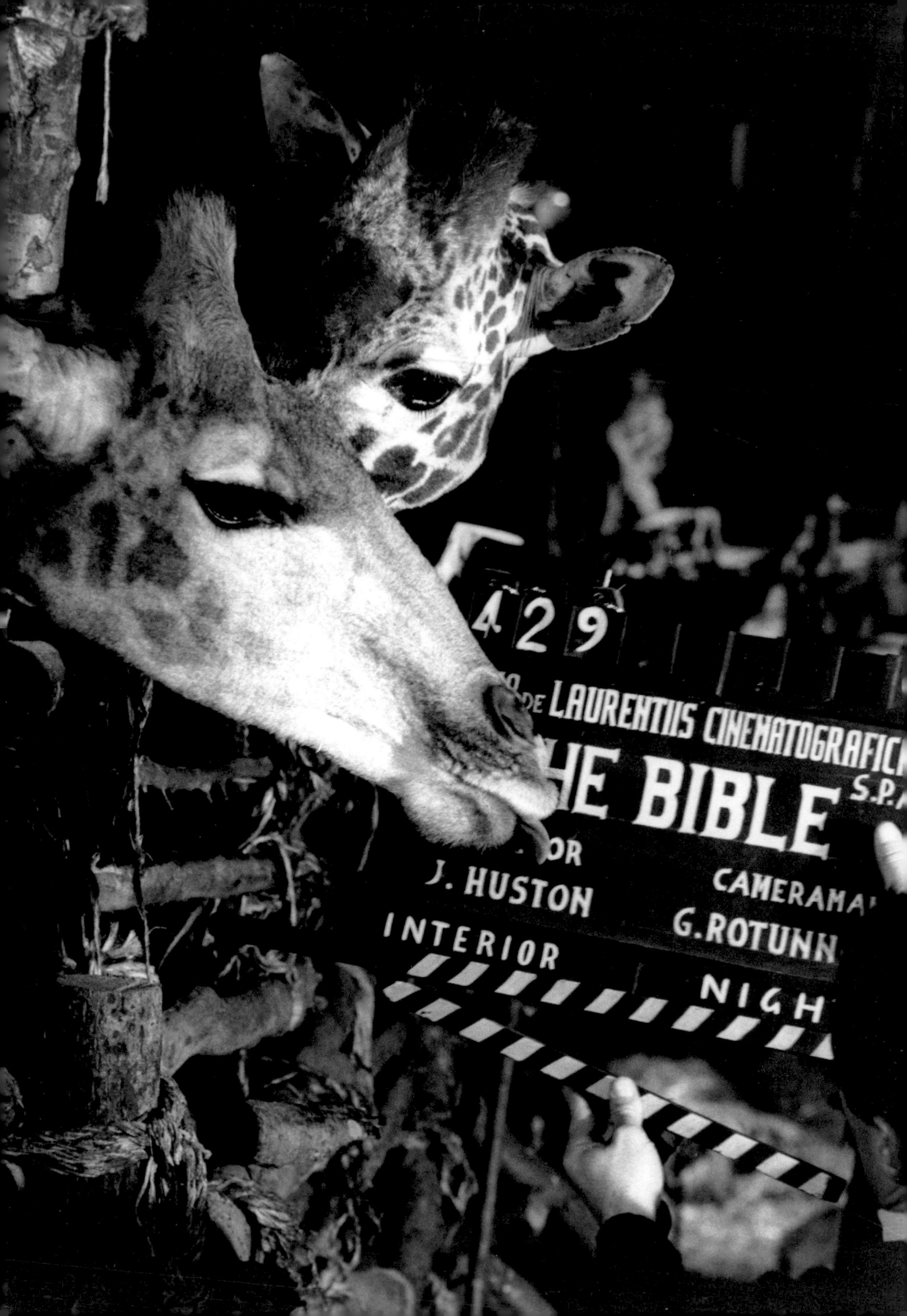
429
DE LAURENTIIS
BIBLE
J. HUSTON
INTERIOR

THE BIBLE

(1965)
1000 birds
300 pairs of animals
Actor/director: John Huston

The film *The Bible* was said to have been financed by an unholy trinity: Hollywood, the Vatican and the Mafia. True or false, it makes a good story.

John Huston invited me to Rome, where he was filming the section on Noah's Ark. He suggested I come for a week to see the three hundred pairs of animals and one thousand birds who were learning to live together in the Ark. He figured that he would have finished the interior shots with the animals by then and that they would be sufficiently accustomed to each other so that he could lead them peaceably into the Ark two by two.

Huston himself was playing Noah. He had wanted to cast Charlie Chaplin or Alec Guinness, but Chaplin refused and Guinness was elsewhere committed. When Huston tried to think of someone of the proper stature and authority, he saw his father, the late Walter Huston. He must then logically have seen himself. A most fastidious man, he started appearing in the Ark unshaven, and as he started acting out scenes with the animals, his beard got longer and longer. There were hazards of birds overhead and elephant dung underfoot. Experienced journalists turned up with plastic hats, plastic macs and wellingtons. When all the animals were in place and the lights blazing, the stench was overpowering. A man walked about with a huge atomizer from which he sprayed a deodorant that

The giraffes get a taste of film-making during filming of the Ark for *The Bible*. Rome, 1965.

Noah (John Huston) commiserates with his friend. Rome, 1965.

anaesthetized one's nostrils, but it was almost worse than the smell. The noise was overpowering, too: the roar of caged tigers, barnyard braying, barking, jungle calls, wild screeching and singing birds. The humans added their babble of tongues: the German trainers' baby talk to their charges; the Italian actress who played Noah's wife learning her lines (in English) from a coach; Huston giving instructions (in English) to his first assistant, who repeated them in Italian to a Danish interpreter, who translated them into German for the actors playing Noah's sons.

When Huston, in sackcloth costume, greeted me, he was patting the dugs of an elephant, who loved the attention. 'I had a nightmare,' he said. 'I dreamed I was directing *The Bible* and I woke up screaming.' He had reason to scream a few days later when he came down with an excruciating attack of gout, and filming had to be stopped. This happened at a propitious time, because Dino De Laurentiis, the producer, had run out of money. Meanwhile the animals had to be fed, and the food bill was enormous.

Even the 'featured' animals who were circus-trained and accustomed to performing found it difficult to get used to the Ark and each other. The first few days after their arrival at the vast compound in the Rome studio, they were ill at ease. The arc lights made the cocks neurotic. Every time the full brilliance came on, they thought it was dawn and crowed wildly. The flamingos were tense and nervous and in danger of breaking their spindly legs if they were startled by a sudden movement. The giraffes were neurotic and worried – until Huston and the trainers hit upon the idea of feeding them sugar lumps mixed with corn as a tranquillizer. As the days stretched into weeks, there were so many interruptions, hold-ups and changes in the production schedule that I decided to do my own two-by-two – just photographing the animals and birds in pairs – because it seemed unlikely that I could spare the time to await the triumphal march into the Ark. Afterwards, when I went to say goodbye to Huston, he was sitting on a bale of hay, dressed in his sackcloth Noah outfit. While Professori, the raven, picked at corn in his hand, he was being interviewed by the religious editor of a French publication: Why is he making *The Bible*? Is it a religious experience? In what way will it differ from other vehicles for bosoms and battles? Whose idea was it that Adam and Eve should be naked?

'God's,' said John Huston.

Two weeks later Huston called me in London. He was jubilant. He had that day led the animals into the Ark two by two. Luckily for him, he decided to shoot through what would normally have been a rehearsal – and all followed him obediently. Then he decided on another take for insurance. This time there was chaos: all the animals refused to budge. That was OK with Huston. He had the scene all carefully locked away in the tin of shadows that was his master copy of *The Bible*.

Noah (John Huston) feeds the hippo. Rome, 1965.

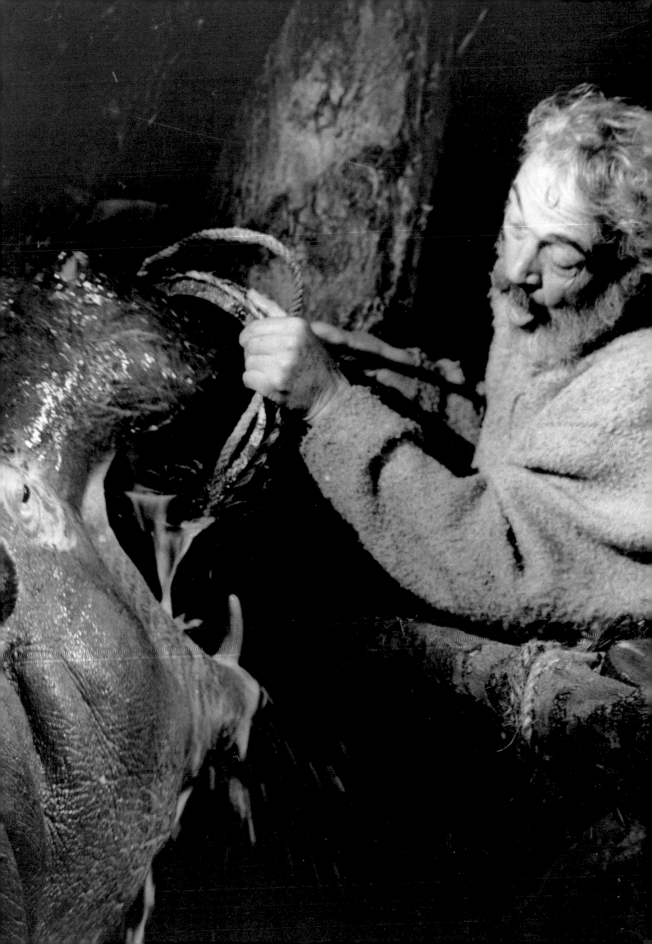

The charladies come to gawk and to cadge lunch. *Life at the Top*. Bradford, England, 1965.

LIFE AT THE TOP

(1965)

Laurence Harvey, Jean Simmons, Honor Blackman
Director: Ted Kotcheff

'Gentlemen, I must ask you once again not to look into the camera. When I say "turn over", look at Miss Blackman.'

Two hundred men have been hired to look at Honor Blackman. They listen courteously to Ted Kotcheff, the director of *Life at the Top*. They are extras playing a scene in Bradford's Wool Exchange. Sixty-five of them work for the Exchange; thirty come from the local labour exchange; most are retired people; one is a reporter on the local paper who wants to get the 'feel of how a film is made – you know, the authentic stuff'; a few are professional actors from London and Manchester; and the balance have been recruited from amateur theatrical groups.

They are all pretty tired and disappointed. They thought it would be exciting, and all they've done is stand around and wait. It doesn't measure up to the films they've seen about Hollywood. Film-making, well, it just isn't glamorous. Maybe if you're Laurence Harvey it's all right. One says his feet hurt. 'It's the toughest day I've put in in five years, and when I go to see the film, I'll blink my eye, and you won't see me.'

Outside, two policemen keep the watching crowd in order. They talk about the extras. 'Some of the men in there are millionaires, and they think it's smashing to earn three quid for the day and have a bash.'

One says, 'Yeah, out there are three extras that I locked up myself this year. One is a con man who hasn't done a bit of work in the last ten years. Must be down on his luck to do this for three quid a day. He must be the one that tried to steal the scene.' They both laugh. 'We're poor brothers here in Bradford. In London they must make films every day, but here this is only the third.'

The charladies who look after the town hall gather to watch the filming. Thirty of them have been coming for morning break and afternoon tea, and eating more than the cast and crew put together. Everybody agrees that the food provided by the movie company is the finest. These are uninvited but appreciative guests. They watch Laurence Harvey make his maiden speech in the town council. One of them sighs, 'It's an experience. We've never been behind the scenes before. Wish they would do it every week.'

Sir Donald Wolfit walks by. He was in the first film, *Room at the Top*, which was also shot in Bradford. Looking at the charwomen, he grins and says, 'It's like the Thirty Years War, it just goes on.'

I went back to source material – my interviews with Simone Signoret and Jean Simmons for the Jack Clayton films I worked on later; the coincidence was both women had worked on the author John Braine's films: *Room at the Top*, which won Simone an Oscar, and *Life at the Top*, which starred Jean Simmons. Also coincidentally they both talked about ageing and the actress's place in films. They agreed that by thirty or thereabouts women are deemed past their prime, men at the peak of their powers. And it is rare, except in character parts, for women to be starred after forty. Men can just go on and on.

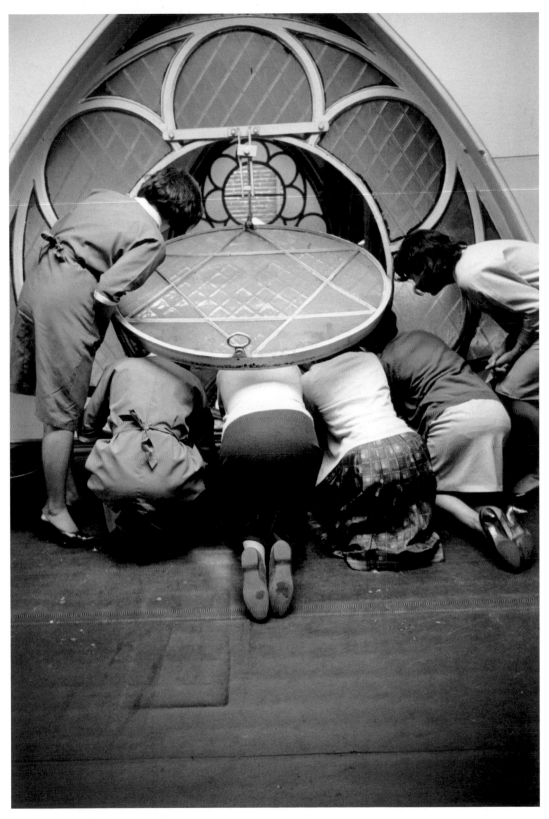

Schoolgirls are playing hooky to watch the making of *Life at the Top*. Bradford, England, 1965.

Retired businessmen and men on welfare are extras at three quid a day. The film is *Life at the Top*, made in Brontë country.
England, 1965.

In the foreground is Laurence Harvey, who plays a recently jumped-up character from the North of England.
Bradford, 1965.

Having made bad jokes with Jean Simmons for weeks and found
she had a fine sense of humour, I tried a bit of irony to kick off
the August 1965 interview. She, to my surprise, took me seriously –
and went on to be serious (and open) during the entire two
hours that we talked.

'Tell me, Jean, what is your philosophy about negligees?'
Jean Simmons looked at the publicist. He shifted his feet, and Jean
said, 'They should be sexy and comfortable.
'You know, ever since I appeared in that nude scene in *Spartacus* in
1958, and the London papers picked it up and started saying things
like "What are they doing to our little girl?" and "Our Jean is being
ruined in the United States", the questions in my interviews have
begun to change.
'You see, they watched me grow up, and I have a sweet image, but
now that image has got to change. I am no longer a little girl. I am
thirty-six years old.
'I never had to make any decisions of any kind. I was just patted on
the head and told to go ahead with my work. Sort of "There, there,
little girl, leave things with older and wiser heads. Don't you worry,
we'll make the decisions for you." That is until I met my husband
Richard. Then he said, "You decide." I had to make my own
decisions – but I still chicken out. Still, I'm always discovering,
oops, I can do it. I've just been late in maturing. I've always had
this feeling of being scared. I wanted to let everybody else be
responsible. It showed in my work as well.
'I was going into a shell. It was mainly Richard, and this old buddy
of mine, Noel Willman, who got me out of it. It was sweet of them.

They said that I was a good actress and should work.

'I thought a bit about my life. It really was too easy. I was turning out films like sausages, one right after another. I had had practically no life except movies. I started when I was fourteen. Bits and pieces. Then at sixteen I was in *Great Expectations*, and that was really the beginning of it. It was a spoilt and artificial life before; all terribly easy and too quick.

'In my wildest dreams I had wanted to be a nightclub performer. I had no thought about films. When I was at ballet school, there was a request for a fourteen-year-old who looked twelve. I read a few lines and was in films.

'Mummy is an unsophisticated creature. One would have thought that she would want to see how movies were made, but she never came on the set at all. Father was a gymnastics instructor. When he was fifty he was doing swan dives and was marvellous. He represented England in 1912 in gymnastics in the Olympics, and got third prize.

'His name was Charles Simmons, but my mother had a marvellous name before her marriage. She was Winifred Ada Loveland. I was called Jean Merilyn Simmons. When I started in films, they wanted to call me Merilyn Loveland, but I got on my high horse. Even at fourteen I thought it was a bit much. I said Simmons was good enough for my father, and good enough for me.

'Growing up, my ambition in life was to be thirty. I wanted to be mature and glamorous, and the age to be was thirty. At thirty, I was getting a divorce. It was a bad time for me. Sad. My marriage broke up, and it was not glamorous. I just worked hard, and I remember particularly the frustration about working.

Jean Simmons, who wants to change her screen image from sweet, young ingénue to a more interesting and substantial woman. *Life at the Top.* Bradford, England, 1965.

'When I married Richard, I wanted to stop work for a while. Perhaps it was all part and parcel of the bad time. Almost it was a struggle to get back into the real world, and out of the fantasy world. That may have made me want to stop. At any rate I did stop, and I had Kate, and things were marvellous, but I was getting restless.

'Richard and I talked about my going back to work. He felt that it was a waste of talent to stay away. I did not want to battle the competition. I wanted to act because I love it. I have no ambition to be number one, or two, or three, or four.

'Now that I am back I feel relaxed, and work is lovely. Part of it must be the security thing. I guess it is being Mrs Richard Brooks. I had always played it safe. I was afraid of making an ass of myself. But now, if I'm asked to do something, I do, and don't worry about what people will think.

'Naturally, I want people to like what I am doing, but I can't wait around to be patted on the head, or kicked in the bottom. This, more than anything else, has helped to take away the fear.

'When I read *Life at the Top*, I thought Susan (the character I play) a mature woman. When Ted Kotcheff (the director) and I talked, he thought her a silly, spoiled, thirty-six-year-old adolescent. I saw her as a bitchy, knowing woman, but he saw her lashing out. A woman who is unloved can be cruel.

'Then I started to think about her and talk about her, and the more I thought, and the more I talked about her to Ted, the more I saw that I knew her too well. It was my real self, and I did not like it, and said, "How dare you cast me in this?"

'It was a shattering thing to face. Ten years ago that would have upset me, but now I just faced it. While playing this silly bitchy creature, one is always digging back and thinking, oops, I know all about that.

'It is a wonderful thing, though, to play a part like this. One gets all sorts of nastinesses out of one's system, and can then go off set and be sweet to everybody. One doesn't have to take it out on anybody else.

'I'm not a constipated actress any more. You know, a poker-up-the-ass type. I haven't seen any work I've done since my so-called growing-up. I'd done only two things that have been released since my marriage to Richard. The film flop *All the Way Home* and the play which folded in Philadelphia – *Rich Little Rich Girl*. The first, I did not want to see, and the second I could not see myself in.

'I'm not objective about my own work. I do not go to rushes, nor even to my finished films. I'm not sure that I can learn from looking at rushes, but I do want to see *Life at the Top* when it is finished. I'm afraid that if I saw rushes now, I would be seeing all the wrong things. You know, like double chins.

'I cannot help but constantly think about that age thing. At thirty you start thinking about being forty, and pushing age. I hope to get it over soon, and then get on with it. I don't know what it is, but in this country, it is as though it is a crime to grow old. As though everybody isn't doing it. Or maybe it is just this business.

'Of course, the one person in the world that I want to please is Richard. If he would say, "It really didn't come off, kid, but I know what you are trying to do," that would be what would matter. It is his understanding, and you go on trying to produce something that will be understood.

'All this stretching and striving is marvellous. It's stimulating, because if one gets into a cosy position and thinks, he's going to love me anyway – although he would – it is much more exciting not to take for granted every minute of the day.

'Now we are talking about work, but this goes into the marriage too. I must go on learning, or I will bog down. Nobody can sit back and think, I've reached the top, and now I'll stay there.

'It just crossed my mind that it is marvellous to be loved as a woman, and respected as an individual, and that this has helped in my growing up. Richard opened the door for me, and I must make sure that I don't close it.

'We're very bad about not being together. In fact, if we don't get together soon, we'll go bankrupt just on telephone calls.

'I know when people ask me questions and I start talking, I sound so sure. But one can only strive and hope. All I know is that I feel safe with Richard, and that being with him, and learning from him, and just the way he treats me gives me confidence.

'I am not sure what he gets from me. I hope it is good.'

Jean Simmons in *Life at the Top*. Bradford, England, 1965.

Richard Brooks, a film director in Hollywood, has come to visit his wife Jean Simmons in England.
She is filming *Life at the Top*. Bradford, England, 1965.

James Stewart in a harrowing make-up session in the desert, which takes a daily three hours to complete.
The film is *The Flight of the Phoenix*. Arizona,1965.

THE FLIGHT OF THE PHOENIX

(1965)
James Stewart, Peter Finch, Richard Attenborough,
Dan Duryea
Director: Robert Aldrich

The winter in London was wet, grey and gloomy. I felt mildewed and longed for the sun, so when 20th Century-Fox called one stormy day, within hours I was on a plane to Arizona to work on *The Flight of the Phoenix*. Here, too, I am lucky to have kept my original writing, which I give here to show the individual way each film differed from the last. My previous one (*Life at the Top*) shot in the North of England differs totally from *The Flight of the Phoenix* shot on the desert sands of Arizona.

Hollywood Sahara by Eve Arnold
Robert Aldrich looked at the men sweeping up the desert (to remove footprints) and shook his head. 'In the old days it was mad dogs and Englishmen, but now it is movie companies and lizards that go out in the noonday sun. OK, boys, let's make it. Hot Line, please.'
He was in the American Sahara, the Californian desert fifteen miles from Yuma, Arizona, directing *The Flight of the Phoenix*, a story of an aeroplane, the flight of fourteen men crash-landed in the desert, and their desperate efforts to survive. They were on their fifth week of shooting, and already seven of the fourteen men in the cast had died or been murdered on schedule. While the survivors were valiantly working in the perishing desert heat which rose to 135

degrees Fahrenheit in the afternoons, the 'dead' men were back in Hollywood keeping cool in swimming pools and waiting for the rest of the company to return so they could shoot the beginning of the picture back at the studio.

The honeymoon that started with the film was almost over, and the cast and crew were tired and homesick, and seeking every bit of available shade. Jimmy Stewart, who plays the part of an ageing pilot, was burrowed into the sand under the nose of the plane. He was waiting to be called for a dawn scene in an open cockpit on which the afternoon sun had been beating. He pulled on his heavy jacket and leather gloves. 'In thirty years I played in seventy pictures. When you consider that each took about twelve weeks, eight hours a day and eighty per cent of the time was spent in lighting, I figure I've been waiting for two and a half years.' The 'brutes' – the big lights – were turned on, and Stewart crawled out of his sand hole to play his scene.

The desert looked like a huge photographic fashion studio, with dunes and sand stretching endlessly like limitless rolls of no-seam paper, a kind of neutral backdrop to the film. In the middle of this vast space stood the wind machines (used to blow up storms) the miles of cables, stepladders, lights, generators, sand buggies, trucks and cars, trailers and toilets (called honey wagons), actors and their stand-ins, and a crew of over two hundred people to do everything from raking the dunes to sewing a seam in a pair of split trousers, cooking hot meals and supplying cold drinks, salt tablets and watermelon.

This desert location has been used almost like a Hollywood back lot. To date, publicists' records being accepted as accurate, twenty-eight films about the Sahara have been made there, and only three in the real Sahara desert. Hollywood goes on the premise that sand is sand, and it looks the same whether it is in Africa or California. Everybody from Rin Tin Tin to Valentino has played in this desert. The cast of characters reads like Grauman's Chinese Theater; Gary Cooper, Marlene Dietrich, Myrna Loy, Ramon Navarro, William Powell, Victor McLaglen, Errol Flynn, Tyrone Power, Cary Grant, Douglas Fairbanks Jr, Humphrey Bogart, James Mason, Sir Cedric Hardwicke, Richard Burton, Boris Karloff, and now James Stewart, with his international cast of colleagues. The films they appeared in range from *The Son of the Sheik* to *Desert Song, Morocco, The Garden of Allah*, two versions of *Beau Geste*, two *Road* pictures (*Road to Zanzibar, Road to Morocco*), to say nothing of innumerable westerns, and one movie called *Old Chicago*. (Did they burn the city down on the desert when Mrs O'Leary's cow went into action, or did they use special effects?)

Stewart comes back from his shot to wait some more. He watches a stills man pose Dan Duryea in a praying position on the burning sand. Aldrich yells, 'Don't waste it, Dan, pray for rain.' Everybody laughs. The make-up man comes over to touch up Stewart's plastic skin.

There are four make-up men on the set. The picture is being shot in sequence, and all the actors have beards. Since they have been exposed to the searing desert and have practically no water (in the film, that is), they are dehydrated, their skins cracked, blistered and broken. All this is done with plastic and make-up.

Stewart, Aldrich, Attenborough and Duryan discuss a scene in the aircraft. Aldrich, to whom a plane is 'where you got on in

Richard Attenborough naps in the noonday sun in the desert. The film is *The Flight of the Phoenix*. Arizona, 1965.

Hollywood and get off in London', listens respectfully while
Stewart, who is a real brigadier general in the Air Corps
Reserve, explains a detail, the nicety of which only another
pilot would understand.

Aldrich nods, sets up to shoot. 'OK, MOS.' A visiting reporter – a
female in shorts and a black umbrella from the local press in Yuma
– wants to know what MOS means. The director explains. A silent
shot. A Hollywood term. Mitout Sound. MOS.

An assistant director calls over a powered megaphone, 'Gunga
Dins.' Two young Mexican lads working their summer vacation
with the picture bring cups of cold water.

It is getting hotter. Somebody has stuck a thermometer into the
sand, and it's registered 150 degrees. The wind has started to blow
sand devils. Shooting stops for a bit, it's blowing too hard to work.
When the men are not talking about home, they're talking about
the sand or the heat. Tomorrow may be better, they'll be working in
a quarry five miles away. And then Hollywood and home.

An old gaffer says, 'I'll be glad to get back to the smog. The
difference between smog and the sand is that you don't have to
wash the smog out of your belly button.'

Robert Aldrich and his dog after an abominable day in the broiling desert.
The film is *The Flight of the Phoenix*. Arizona, 1965.

Martin Ransohoff, who produced Steve McQueen's film *The Cincinnati Kid*. Hollywood, 1961.

Terence Stamp and his then girlfriend Jean Shrimpton, top sixties model, dress up for the opening night of
Modesty Blaise. London, 1965.

Terence Stamp and Monica Vitti clown it up for the still camera. They are recording music for *Modesty Blaise*. London, 1965.

MODESTY BLAISE

(1965)
Terence Stamp, Monica Vitti, Dirk Bogarde
Director: Joseph Losey

The director Joe Losey steps up to the camera, calls 'Action' and as he directs his star, Monica Vitti, she moves in the opposite direction from the instructions she was given at rehearsal. Losey looks behind him and sees Michelangelo Antonioni over his shoulder directing Miss Vitti with body gestures.

Miss Vitti has a problem. She has been told that she is ugly in profile, that she looks like a housemaid in profile, so she is countermanding her director's instructions and taking direction from her lover, who has directed all her Italian films. This is her first American film. Losey plays it cool, keeps on filming, but somehow that half-hour is the only time Antonioni is seen on set. The obsession about her profile goes deep. Although she has a Nefertiti nose, she is convinced it's ugly and I get instructions from Miss Vitti: no profiles. The prohibition makes photographing her difficult, because the injunction of no profiles inhibits us both. We have to keep imposing the stricture instead of being free. Yet despite everything, the idea of the film is an amusing one and Monica is a comic in the mode of Marilyn Monroe and she clowns the session to make the film fun.

Modesty Blaise is the story of a glamorous superspy who can outfight and outfox anyone and remain completely feminine. It is based on a syndicated comic strip and is a combination of action, sex and pop art.

Terence Stamp: dressing room, Royal Opera House. *Modesty Blaise*. London, 1965.

Monica Vitti during filming of *Modesty Blaise*. Sicily, 1965.

Monica Vitti has gone from filming in a blonde wig to a dark hairdo. *Modesty Blaise*,
Royal Opera House dressing room. London, 1965.

Terence Stamp in *Modesty Blaise* has gone from dark to light wig. Royal Opera House dressing room.
London, 1965.

Its plot revolves around a fortune in diamonds that has been promised by the British government to an Arab sheikh in exchange for oil concessions. The problem is to transmit the diamonds safely to the sheikh.

For her part, Modesty (Monica Vitti) has a miniature arsenal: a lipstick that telescopes into a poisoned arrow, a perfume atomizer that sprays compressed air, gold buttons on her dress that become retractable pins that kill on impact, and a ring that turns into a flashlight. The zany adventuress is a two-dimensional comicstrip send-up of James Bond.

I realized when I was working with Monica Vitti how different my interviews with movie stars were. I was with them for long stretches of time, I could observe them, talk to them, earn their trust during working hours as well as social hours. If I put this way of working against the set-up formal interview which is limited in time to hours, I realize just how fortunate I was in my dealings with film people.

Michelangelo Antonioni directing *Blow-Up*. London, 1965.

Vanessa Redgrave with her daughters Joely and Natasha. London, 1966.

Vanessa Redgrave at her dressing table about to prepare for opening night of *The Prime of Miss Jean Brodie*. London, 1966.

Simone Signoret in her hotel room at the Savoy. She is to play an unglamorous widow and to be murdered in a John le Carré film *The Deadly Affair*. London, 1966.

The Deadly Affair

(1966)
Simone Signoret, James Mason
Director: Sidney Lumet

It is a normal day's work for Simone Signoret. She is to be murdered in the stalls of a London theatre, but in between takes she will be interviewed for television, photographed for magazines, questioned by newspapers, speak in English, French, German and Italian to the foreign press. She chats with a friend while she waits for the next reporter: 'They always ask the same four basic questions: sex, money, age and work, and the order changes depending on who is asking the questions.'

Sidney Lumet is directing her in a spy thriller, *The Deadly Affair*, a John le Carré film in which she plays the part of a Nazi concentration-camp victim, a fifty-year-old Jewish woman in England whose husband is found dead. Lumet has set himself the impossible task of deglamorizing her. She wears heavy braids, dowdy clothes, clodhopper shoes, but even in these props the expressive blue-green eyes, the sexy long legs, the wonderful feminine mouth are still there. She is still unmistakably all woman and generates enormous appeal.

She sits in the stalls of the theatre, surrounded by hundreds of extras who play the audience. On stage, Lumet is setting the scene for the next shot. While Simone will be getting hers in the stalls, David Warner as Edward II will be killed on stage. A Marlowe play within the film. Camera crew, grips, electricians, carpenters and

151

painters move about among the Elizabethan-costumed actors. Lumet is everywhere at the same time. Simone watches all this activity and starts to talk to a man from the local newspaper. She will be as patient with him as with the man from the BBC – poised and utterly professional. And inevitably there *are* the same four questions. She talks with humour and spontaneity, and has a fresh and different answer for each.

'Listen. Forty is not something you catch, like a disease. It's not the flu. If the twenty years which precede it haven't been filled with life, with joy and love and tears, then waking up suddenly at forty must be a terrible experience for a woman. But if those years have been filled to the brim, then it's nothing. And certainly not fatal. Too many women seem to feel it's the age when they have to retreat from the war. There's a war going on, you know, between men and women, but I have never belonged to that army. I'm a deserter, so don't use me as an example. I'm not against men, I'm for them. I'm much more inclined to believe a man who cries than a woman. I'm always very suspicious of a woman's tears. And women who talk about sacrifice, about what they've given up for a man – ugh! It's nonsense, a lie. When you do something for someone else rather than yourself, you're doing it for one reason – to please yourself. Everyone is free, after all.

'I've played some real bitches in my time. When you are young, you can play handsome girls. After that, for a woman of my age, you must play character parts. They are much more interesting to do. To be honest, you've got to play them anyway, so you'd better find them interesting!

'And if you are really honest – well; in this film I'm making, she is a

James Mason clutching his script of *The Deadly Affair*. London, 1966.

woman of fifty, an absolute wreck – it is terrible to see. She has nothing; absolutely no femininity at all. I have seen the rushes and I pretend I don't mind. I am above all an actress.

'One has to live life with its joys and its sadness, its good things and its bad, its pleasures and its disasters. I learned a long time ago that there is no substitute for living. You cannot show emotion unless you have experienced it or real passion unless you truly feel it.

'I think that constantly spending your days working on your face, your figure and your bank account so that even your husband has to make an appointment to see you is no life.

'How much does financial independence have to do with being able to choose one's roles? Is it possible to be indiscriminate on the way up and then assert your conscience once you've got to the top? I'm very suspicious of this view. Once you start, you can't stop. First it is to pay the rent. Then there's the little house in the country. Then the pool. Then the pool must be heated. It's like the man who does illustrations and says one day he'll paint his masterpiece. It's a load of crap.

'Problems help to keep you young. Years ago, one had a friend. That friend would listen to your worries. But try to find someone to do that nowadays. The only person who will do it is a psychiatrist. You have to buy the time that used to be given free. Nowadays nobody wants to have problems on their hands, particularly someone else's. They want life easy; clean, clinical, like oven-ready chickens, packaged with the guts taken out and the head removed. Nothing dirty. But they're missing so much. It's wonderful to have problems. It's creative.

'There have been tragedies among people who have sought to be big stars. But you don't think it is because they have tried so hard that they have not had time to live. I have always lived my life to the full.

'While I am working, work is all. I cannot understand actors and actresses who film and then think about shopping and going out to dinner. While I am making a film I wish they would lock us all up together until we had finished.

'There are three things to consider in deciding on a role: the director, the story and the role itself. I don't want to give them first place and second place – they are all married together. A good director? Someone you trust because you love the work he has done. Story? It can be on any level: a thriller, a social drama, a love story, but always something you believe in. I don't mind playing an unsympathetic part if I believe in the film.

'Creating a role is a mysterious process – like growing angry or making love. You read a script and if you're really hooked at once – that's it. Otherwise it's no good. And there she is, the character you're going to play. You don't know her yet completely, but she's all there on paper. Your first meeting with her is the only important occasion. After that you don't think about it, but she begins to grow. You see somebody in the street, you notice some little mannerism, an expression. Something connects. Her clothes, her hair. These are not so important but the picture keeps getting filled in. The period when the film is to be made is getting nearer all the time, then suddenly, she's given birth! She's there!'

Madame Signoret moves between being filmed and being interviewed. During the week it took to shoot the murder sequences, she had answered hundreds of questions, but she was wrong when she spoke of only four categories of questions. There was a fifth, which dealt with her being a mother. She said to the friend she had talked to on the first day in the theatre, 'When a woman runs away with a man and already has a child by another, she is lucky if the man loves the child. I was lucky when I ran away with Montand. Maybe it worked so well because I had a girl. They love each other, and we are a very close family.'

She talked about Catherine Allégret, her nineteen-year-old daughter who played a girl in a brothel scene where she walks across the camera in the film *Lady L* with Sophia Loren. Catherine was very much impressed, Simone says. She had met a real movie star!

'She [Catherine] is not wide-eyed about the [film] business like so many young girls. She knows a first night is more than just pretty dresses; it is also a sort of death for the actress; the "corrida". But I admit it, I am proud of her, and she looks like me.

'A mother has only five things to teach her daughter: to brush her hair, to clean her teeth, to share her cake with her friends at school, to tell as few lies as possible and last – well, you don't have to believe in Little Jesus to get the point – that an Italian isn't a "macaroni", an Arab isn't a "wop" and a Negro isn't a "nigger". That's a base, isn't it, a good beginning?'

And yes, there was the sixth question, the one that was perhaps number one in each reporter's mind, and the one that very few dared ask: the one about Marilyn Monroe and Montand. (Montand had been carrying on an affair with Monroe.) About this nothing was answered except to the friend.

'What troubled me most in this situation was the roles we were forced into by the press. Each one of us was assigned a part. Marilyn was the blond seductress, Yves the seducer, Miller the wronged husband, and [here she drew a halo around her head with her fingers] I became Joan of Arc.'

She went back to play the final shot of her murder scene. 'I'm going to "die" happily. Why shouldn't I? I have my Oscar, some money, some love and some success. Can one ask more?'

Sophia Loren with Charles Chaplin, who directs her in *A Countess from Hong Kong.* He enjoyed her enormously.
England, 1966.

A COUNTESS FROM HONG KONG

(1966)
Sophia Loren, Marlon Brando
Director: Charles Chaplin

The day I came to the studio to photograph Charlie Chaplin for a cover for *Newsweek*, the unit publicist briefed me: 'Fifteen minutes is all the time Charlie will allow.' Fifteen minutes for a cover? He had to be joking. No, he wasn't. Fifteen or nothing. I gulped – said, 'I suppose I have no choice, I'll take it.' Since every second would count, could I have recce time? Would they at least let me check out the situation, observe from a distance, become familiar with the lighting, see how Charlie moved? Could I hang around for a morning? All this so I could maximize my fifteen minutes.

'OK,' said the publicist, 'but don't trip over the cables.'

With this dubious blessing I was on my own, cursing my bad luck. I stood in the shadows watching the small darting figure that was Charlie Chaplin set up a shot. I kept telling myself, I know he's seventy-seven years old, but why doesn't he look like the *Little Tramp* of my youth? Here was this ancient with a hat whose brim was meant to protect his eyes that were covered by thick, thick glasses. The little paunch, too, was disappointing. Damn! How was I to show the man who was a film immortal, a legend who gave the world so much pleasure by being the butt of so many of life's calamitous little jokes? But as I stood watching, suddenly there was a magical moment. Chaplin danced and the world was transformed. I gasped. Chaplin stopped dancing, turned to Sophia Loren and Marlon Brando and said, 'That's the way I want you both to dance.' Then he motioned to an assistant director and indicated that he wanted his footsteps chalked up so his actors could duplicate his steps.

It was all so rigid, as was the camerawork. He simply did not move the camera – which worried the crew – but to the actors it was OK. After all, he was Chaplin. He had thought up the screenplay, written the music, and now he was their director. Hats off to him. All over the stage one felt this homage to an innovator, a major figure – so when he couldn't remember Brando's first name and referred to him as 'hey, you' or as 'Marlo', it was OK with Brando. He stood in awe of the old man and took directions no matter what he might have thought of them. With Sophia Chaplin was flirty and gallant. Today was his seventy-seventh birthday. He looked at Sophia with a twinkle and said, 'Oh, to be seventy again!' Meanwhile, the publicist had a bright idea, since the idea of age was in the air. While I was lurking in the shadows, he showed Chaplin the issue of the *Sunday Times* that showed the centenarians in the Caucasus that I had photographed: five hundred men over a hundred years old from Sachumi to Baku – all hale. For me All hail!, because Chaplin was passionately anxious to make it over the hundred-mark and allegedly lived in Switzerland near a gland specialist who injected him with monkey-gland serum to prolong life.

The publicist then led me over to the maestro, the fifteen-minute injunction was forgotten, and I was invited to take my time and was permitted to come back on the morrow and for three days running. Each day I was quizzed about the old men. On the first

Marlon Brando in *A Countess from Hong Kong*. England, 1966.

day, it was 'What was their diet like, what did they eat?' On the second day, exercise was in question. On the third day, when I already had the cover at the processor's, he wanted to know how many times – presumably he meant sex.

Before I left, I saw him dance once more. It was magic. He didn't need those monkey glands, his dancing was sheer bliss. Sadly, no mere photo could record the beauty, the grace. He was the *Little Tramp* all over again. Bravo!

Charles Chaplin directing *A Countess from Hong Kong* on his seventy-seventh birthday. That morning he looked at Sophia Loren and said, 'Oh, to be seventy again!' England, 1966.

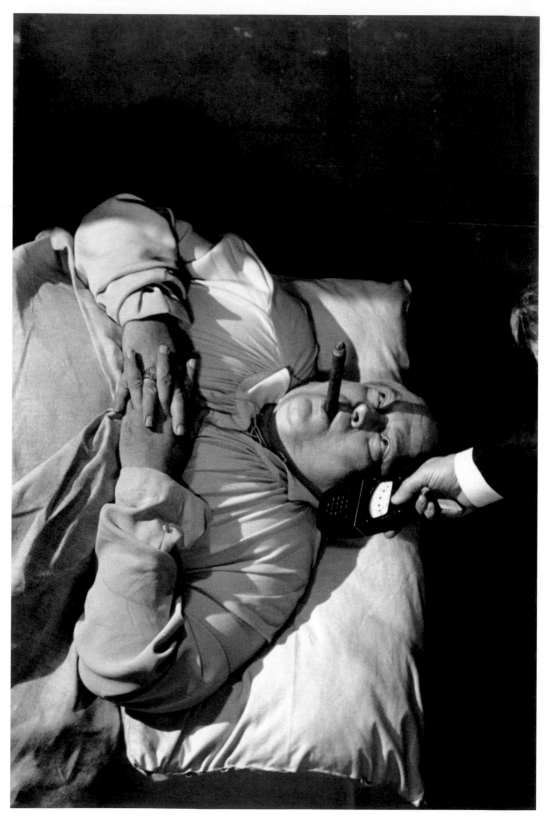

Orson Welles plays the dying Cardinal Wolsey. He smokes his Havana cigar while all about him are preparing for a 'take'. *A Man for All Seasons*. England, 1966.

A MAN FOR ALL SEASONS

(1966)
Paul Scofield, Orson Welles
Director: Fred Zinnemann

Paul Scofield was playing a highly emotional scene with Orson Welles, Scofield on camera with Welles feeding him lines. This was Scofield's close-up, but every time Welles, off camera, was to feed Scofield a line, he, Welles, fluffed the line and they had to begin all over again. Watching Welles from the vantage point of darkness (he, of course, was not lit – it was Scofield's close-up), I was convinced that Welles was deliberately trying to unsettle Scofield. They went through innumerable takes with Scofield urbane and courteous and Welles persisting in missing his lines until even he had had enough and he came through and they could continue shooting. Next time it was Welles's close-up, and Zinnemann and Scofield made sure it was done in two takes.

Welles was endlessly sparring for the superior position: he had the biggest dressing room on the lot, and even though it was only three city blocks from the sound stage, he insisted he have the biggest, most lavish Rolls-Royce to transport him.

I shall never forget his off-camera performance during the three days he threw his weight around as Cardinal Wolsey – or was it as Orson Welles? During his rehearsal for his death scene (which I shot from a gantry sixty feet in the air so as not to distract him), he is lying like a beached whale on a cot. He's wearing a white sacklike garment and is puffing a huge expensive cigar while adjustments of lighting are going on and an assistant is reading the light. I was impressed with Fred Zinnemann throughout all these shenanigans. He simply appeared to ignore them. What a man!

Orson Welles and his limousine. England, 1966.

Dr Dolittle

(1966)
Rex Harrison, Anthony Newley, Samantha Eggar
Director: Richard Fleischer

Once upon a time an officer in the Irish Guards sat in the trenches in France. His heart was sick with seeing not only the suffering of the men about him, but the terror of the cavalry horses, the pigeons, dogs and other animals recruited for the war. To keep his sanity and to keep contact with his children, he wrote letters home making up stories about a compassionate doctor who devoted his life to sick animals, and whose name was Dr Dolittle.

The children wanted to know what their hero looked like, so he added illustrations. These showed a round, tubby, lovable little man with a gentle face, a bulbous nose, a pair of spectacles and a top hat. The man who wrote these stories was Hugh Lofting, and when he returned from the war, he found that his wife had saved all the letters and illustrations. These became the basis for books that generations of children loved and grew up with.

Now, forty-five years later, Chee Chee the monkey, Dab Dab the duck, Gub Gub the pig, Polynesia the parrot, Sophie the seal, a horse called Toggle who wears bifocals, chickens, foxes, lions, crocodiles, giraffes, forty domestic cats, scores of birds, hundreds of sheep and the Pushmi-Pullyu have moved into a new Puddleby on the Marsh.

20th Century-Fox, complete with publicity fanfare, is making a large-scale musical about the little doctor. The elegant Rex Harrison

Shortly, Dr Dolittle (Rex Harrison) will be singing to the sheep.
Castle Combe, England, 1966.

is Dr Dolittle, Anthony Newley is the cat's-meat-man, William Dix
is Tommy Stubbins. And a girl has been added. Samantha Eggar
plays the girl. In typical Hollywood fashion, no expense will be
spared, and costs are said to be greater than the budgets many small
countries allow themselves per year. Reports range between £3
million and £10 million.

Ironically, the film too started with bombs. In the quiet inland
village of Castle Combe in Wiltshire, attempts were made by
zealous patriots to blow up the sea wall built by the film company
to represent a shipping harbour. But since the setting is a seaport,
why not shoot it at a seaside location?

No, sir, says Arthur Jacobs, producer. What do you think he is, some
kind of nut? 'At the seashore we would have tides. The water level
would constantly change, limiting our working time to an hour a
day. High waves would ruin our sets. Fog would delay us. The roar
of breakers would blister our soundtrack. And those seagulls –
squawking when they should keep quiet!' He adds, 'We came to
Castle Combe because we wanted authenticity.'

To make for further 'authenticity', TV antennas have been ripped
down, telephone poles have been removed (and installed in
underground lines to central community antennas outside the
town), and rubber cobblestones are unrolled every morning and
rolled up every night.

Of course, the press has made much of these changes, but in fact
the owner of the stream where the sea wall was built is delighted
with it and feels that it has enhanced his property; the removal of
the antennas and poles help the look of the thousand-year-old
village, and the rubber cobblestones will go back to Hollywood.

This is a typical day's shooting for director Richard Fleischer, if he is not rained out. Rex Harrison, with Polynesia the parrot sitting on his top hat (there is a band stretched across the top of it so that she can sit comfortably), will be talking to two hundred sheep. Harrison originally carried Polynesia on his shoulder, but she nipped him. She did not break the skin – but parrot fever can be fatal. The trainer claims that a parrot uses its beak to steady itself, and that the parrot had gone off balance and grazed Harrison's cheek. Be that as it may, Harrison now carries Polynesia on his hat or on his wrist.

People keep asking him whether he isn't concerned about kids and animals stealing his scenes. 'No,' he says. 'If they do, it is up to the actor to steal them back.' Besides, one notices that when he does carry Polly on his wrist, he easily places her downstage.

When the actors are outnumbered by the animals, as in this case, it is easier for the actor to get the sympathy of the audience. If there were a single cat or dog, the trainers say, the actors would be in trouble. But in this case the actor is the underdog.

There are thirty-seven trainers in Castle Combe. The head trainers are American, and have been augmented by complete zoos and circuses. But alas, the weather has done them in, and but for key scenes that must be filmed in Castle Combe, the circus sequences will be shot on a ranch in California.

Each featured animal has its own stand-in, understudy and dummy. Since no animal can work more than six hours without fatigue, and since the reward for performance is food, if there are retakes, at the end of three pounds of fish for the seal, for example, Sophie is ready for her siesta. So the animals must be carefully handled.

The stand-in is used for light positioning, and the understudy
is available in case the number-one animal is indisposed.
Animals have screen tests like starlets. They either have it or they
do not. Some are clever at tricks, but may be dull on screen. For
instance, the number-three seal is too hammy. She cannot be
disciplined for close-ups. Since she insists upon doing her own
bit for the camera, she will be used in the circus scenes with
other animals.

Filming animals is an unpredictable business, and so the
instructions in the script will read simply, 'Make the swans react.'
In this particular case a scene of Dolittle with the swans was shot
twenty times, each time the trainers trying to get the swans to wag
their tails, using persuasion, food and noise. Each time nothing
happened. On the twentieth take, Fleischer, who kept the cameras
running, yelled, 'Swans, react!' and they sailed by Harrison swishing
their tails in the air. Why? Nobody knew.

Then there was the problem with the ducks. They started to drown,
and had to be rescued. Apparently they were so young, they still
didn't know how to swim.

At first the sheep sequences caused a great deal of difficulty.
Fleischer woke in the middle of the night and had the answer.
His problem was to show the sheep looking at Harrison with their
heads up. He reasoned that there were two causes for them to have
their heads down: when they were bothered by flies, and when they
were nibbling on the grass. He had the sheep brought early in the
morning to the spot where he would shoot. He kept them there
until they had eaten up all the grass, and then sprayed them (and
Harrison) with insecticide. It worked. Harrison talked and sang to

Dr Dolittle has had his problems with Polynesia. Castle Combe, England, 1966.

the animals; they looked at him soulfully.

'That's a miracle shot,' said Fleischer. Came a voice from the sound truck: 'Mr Fleischer, sir, we don't have it on sound. There's a break in the connection somewhere.'

When the seals were filmed, Fleischer again got his 'miracle' shot. They found Sophie moving her head from side to side watching Harrison. She wasn't acting for that fish that was to be her payment, she was moving her head to try and remove the pink lacy hat that she hated so.

Although the audience will see only one Gub Gub the pig, there are at least six pigs ordered for the Hollywood scenes. They scheduled one pig for 20 September, one for the 27th, etc. They grow so fast. Strangely enough, the pigs are the most difficult for Harrison to hold. He says they feel like blocks of iron and kick too hard. Meanwhile, back in the sixteenth-century house where the publicists work, the mill grinds on and the puns and gags about the animals and the actors go out to a waiting world. Fleischer is quoted as having said about a herd of cows that wandered unwanted into a scene, 'Since they've horned in, we'll use them. Let's milk them for all it's worth.' A townsman is quoted as saying, 'How udderly amazing, these Americans. They refuse to be cowed.'

By now it is common knowledge that film-making is a boring process, and the more boring, the more fooling around takes place to lighten the atmosphere. Here, Anthony Quinn and Anna Karina fool around on *The Magus*. Mallorca, 1967.

THE MAGUS

(1967)
Anthony Quinn, Michael Caine, Candice Bergen,
Anna Karina
Director: Guy Green

It was hot in Mallorca; little clusters of foreign reporters sat around interviewing stars of the film on location. Anthony Quinn continued his description of the film. 'It's a generous mixture of mythology and sex.'

In another group, Candice Bergen was saying to an English interviewer, 'Bizarre human chess game.'

An English publicist with an English-speaking Spanish reporter in tow, who was waiting his turn to talk to Michael Caine, was saying, 'It's a mystery thriller.'

Anna Karina was being photographed and interviewed at the same time by *Jour de France*. She was shrugging her shoulders and laughing. 'It's a love story,' she said.

Michael Caine, meanwhile, was surrounded by the German press. Sitting quietly in the background was a little old Belgian lady who had come from Belgium to interview him. She listened to the Germans asking him tough personal questions which he either carried off with Cockney quips or shrugged off. She sat through it all and made notes. When Michael was finally summoned to continue the shooting, the little lady asked the age-old question, 'And Mr Caine, what do you fear most?' The Cockney voice came back, 'Death – what else? Where do you go from there?'

On any film location, anywhere, it is always difficult to sort out

More fooling around. Candice Bergen and Michael Caine try out a tango to pass the time. Mallorca, 1967.

fantasy from reality, the true from the make-believe. But on this set it's even more difficult. One's only defence in trying to get things sorted out is to go back to the book, by John Fowles.

John says, in his interview:

'The basic idea in *The Magus* is to get an idea of modern twentieth-century life. You know, science is killing mystery, and I wanted to maintain that feeling that it's marvellous to be drawn in, to be drawn on not knowing where you are going but knowing that you must follow through.

'The character of Nicholas [played by Michael Caine] is meant to be a kind of every modern man, confused, and looking for something he does not know. Always afraid to make a commitment to himself, or to life.'

Critics of the book have called it 'sheerest fantasy', 'terrifying, tantalizing', 'grotesque persons, fantastic incidents', 'a new experience in a new dimension of writing'.

The massacre scene of the first day's shooting is only one of the strange evocations from the past that occur in the film, being shot on a primative, rock-bound beach in Mallorca. It stars Anthony Quinn as the 'magician', Michael Caine as the young man who is drawn step by step into his web of mystery and evil, Candice Bergen as Lily-Julie, the girl from Quinn's past and Caine's present, and Anna Karina as Caine's link with the outside world. The theme is a struggle for supremacy between the men and a voyage of self-discovery for the younger.

The mood on the film is light-hearted, and the actors fool around – as actors do on any film if things are going well. Candice Bergen and Michael Caine tango for the fun of it. The dance is not in the film.

The final dip in the last step of the tango as Candice Bergen and Michael Caine demonstrate it. Mallorca, 1967.

Anjelica Huston trying out a crying scene. With Anjelica is her father John Huston, who is directing her in *A Walk with Love and Death*. Austria, 1968.

A WALK WITH LOVE AND DEATH

(1968)
Anjelica Huston, Assaf Dayan
Director: John Huston

In 1968, when John Huston decided to make a film with his daughter Anjelica, called *A Walk with Love and Death*, he called me to ask me to photograph her. 20th Century-Fox didn't know her, was uncertain of the way she would photograph and wanted to see pictures of her.

I was third down the list. Cecil Beaton and David Bailey had photographed her before me. In their pictures, although she looked glamorous, she looked too old; the part called for a fourteen-year-old. The studio bosses would sit still for adding a few years, but it wouldn't do to present them with the soignée lady the photographers depicted.

When John called, my first question was, had they used colour or black-and-white? It was black-and-white, which, with the dramatic lighting used, added years. Anjelica was then sixteen and caught between her mother's wish for her to get her A-levels and her father's wish for her to learn to become a film actress. To make matters worse, she had cut off her hair, which had hung way past her shoulders. This, too, made her look older.

Somehow a photographic session got organized. Gladys Hill, John's assistant, managed a wig and a hair piece from Alexandre, the movie stars' hairdresser in Paris. I got Ricky, Anjelica's mother, involved, so she provided an Empire-line dress that was youthful

and romantic. Anjelica and I then flew to Ireland to St Clarens
to photograph.

I thought that with colour film, soft Irish ambience, a ruined castle
on the grounds of John's country manor, we had a chance.

The film is about a medieval troubadour, a Sorbonne dropout, and
his high-born lady-love. The year is 1358, and the story is set
against the background of war and rebellion. The idea was to evoke
comparison with the youth rebellion going on in the present in
France. In fact, while the film was being cast, the barricades went
up in Paris and the students were throwing paving stones.

It was raining when we arrived at St Clarens, which meant we
would have to work indoors. Over lunch, John asked us what kind
of pictures we planned. I told him that it's a bad idea to talk about
pictures beforehand – it tends to rob both photographer and subject
of spontaneity. For me, a thoroughly planned photograph seems to
rule out ideas engendered during the photographing, because the
original idea hijacks the sitting, leaving no space for improvisation.
The photographer has to be able to take advantage of accidents that
occur. For that an almost blank mind – like a blank canvas – is
essential. The idea is to set the place and the time of day, surround
oneself with whatever props are necessary and then proceed.

The subject and photographer, sometimes even without words
between them, then are free to create the essential bond that
makes the image.

I also felt that all the talk might make Anjelica nervous, so I told
Huston he had a nervous photographer on his hands – no talk,
please. He understood immediately and we spoke of other things.
Next day the sun shone. We worked out of doors. Anjelica came

through: young, lovely and vulnerable. We flew back to London, I to process the film, Anjelica to get back to her studies. When the pictures were shown to the studio people, they were enthusiastic. I was then asked to go to Austria to work on the film.

When the student rebellion erupted in France, the originally planned Dordogne venue had to be abandoned. Huston was lucky to find a new set of fourteenth-century castles without losing too much time. We worked in the Vienna Woods, Castle Lichtenstein, a *Naturpark*, and surrounding castles. We were shooting in public parks and it was funny to see the natives on a holiday walk in the Wienerwald brought up short when they encountered the machinery and matériel which follow a film unit, and people talking English, French, Italian and German – it was a polyglot cast and crew. The scene of giant lights, castles, medieval costumes (Assaf and Anjelica), and the three greyhounds who got bored with acting must have been startling but what intrigued the trippers most was Huston directing in his impeccably tailored Italian cape, Irish cap and English boots.

The natives out on their holiday walk looked pretty funny themselves: Papa in lederhosen, Mama in dirndl, their children dressed like Mama and Papa. The families were outfitted with picnic baskets, rugs, alpenstocks, cameras, sun glasses, the lot.

John Huston had directed his father Walter, his son Tony, himself and now it was Anjelica's turn. He said the choice of Anjelica was pure nepotism.

The film was ill-starred. Assaf Dayan's accent was against him, Anjelica was inexperienced, and not even Huston's great skill could save the picture. It was released briefly, just for a few days in New York, then quietly faded away.

John and Anjelica Huston at St Clarens, the manor house in Eire they called home. Ireland, 1968.

Anjelica Huston demonstrates a head-stand for her father, John Huston. She is sixteen years old. Ireland, 1968.

John Huston feeds the hounds. *A Walk with Love and Death*. Austria, 1968.

Anouk Aimée, reviewing her lines before a shot. *Justine*. Tunisia, 1968.

JUSTINE

(1968)
Anouk Aimée, Dirk Bogarde, Michael York
Director: started with Joseph
Strick, then changed to George Cukor

The camels were getting restless, the director was cursing the wind which kept blowing the sand into the cameras; the cameramen were raging because the sun kept going behind the clouds and making it impossible to shoot; the lighting people were busily lighting up the desert with seven huge 'brutes' (klieg lights) to try to match the take of the day before. The generator supplying the power for all this was purring madly; native labourers were planting fully grown stalks of corn in the pomegranate grove; 'grips' were busily sweeping down the dunes to cover footprints made by the people who were lighting the location.

All this surrealist activity for yet another Hollywood film being made in the desert in Tunis by 20th Century-Fox. The film was *Justine*, a $7 million production of the Lawrence Durrell *Alexandria Quartet*: *Justine, Balthazar, Mountolive* and *Clea*. 20th bought all four books for $50,000 and spent eight years and $750,000 developing them into a single narrative. The story is placed in the city of Alexandria in Egypt in 1935. Joe Strick, the director (later replaced by George Cukor), thought that Tunis 1968 was closer to Alexandria 1935 than Alexandria 1968.

The star of the film, playing Justine, is Anouk Aimée, who hit the international film screens with a surprisingly simple low-budget French film called *A Man and a Woman*. Dirk Bogarde plays

Pursewarden, Michael York plays the narrator Darley, John Vernon
plays Nassim, Robert Forster plays Narouz and Anna Karina
plays Melissa.

So there is an international cast, American financing, a Cadillac
bought from the Vatican, a Rolls-Royce shipped from England,
electrical equipment sent from Rome, typewriters brought from
Hollywood, as are miles of cable, stepladders, trailer trucks and
toilets in special trailers. There is a crew of over two hundred people
gathered from Hollywood, Paris, London. They are augmented by
local talent, extras, handymen, musicians and grips from Tunis.
There is also a kitchen crew to supply Cokes with Arabic calligraphy
on them.

The clothes for Anouk Aimée are mainly based on the idea of the
djellaba, a loose, full-length garment done Arabic style in
magnificent silks in whites, blacks and beiges. At the end of the
picture when Justine reverts to being a whore, Miss Sharaff, the
designer, added very ornate gold embroidery to a beige djellaba. The
scene in which she wears this dress was photographed in a palatial
Moorish house that belongs to the Baron Derlanger and is called
Star of Venus.

There were scenes shot in the Medina (the ancient city), in the
souks (bazaars), in the desert, at the seashore, in *feluccas* (sailboats),
in a Bedouin encampment, in a seven-hundred-year-old fort, and in
Takrouna, a town perched on a mountaintop very much like the
Native American pueblo towns in which the inhabitants live in
caves cut into the rocks in the sides of the mountain. Wherever the
cameras appeared, suddenly there were Tunisians of all ages.
Barefoot children, veiled women, curious men in traditional dress.

It would have been interesting to know what they made of all this outlandish show – these people who had been invaded by successive waves of Venetians, Romans, Vandals, French and American tourists. The glory that was Carthage lies within the shadow of the city of Tunis.

One day in the desert miles from anywhere a small group of Tunisians stood by watching the whole complex business of a man with a megaphone trying to whip some artificial light, camera and crew, actors, wardrobe people, make-up artists and hairdressers into a day's work for three believable minutes on screen that an audience would see a year hence somewhere in Idaho. We wondered where they all came from and how they had found us. When we had got through to the interpreter in our mangled French and he had asked the people in Arabic and got back to us in his mangled English, the answer was simple. They said, 'We just followed the cables.'

While the uninvited guests watched the preparations for a scene, I talked to Dirk Bogarde about Anouk Aimée, whom I was to photograph that afternoon. I had made friends with Dirk when I worked on *Our Mother's House* and then on *Modesty Blaise*. I wanted a clue to Anouk's personality and I knew that Dirk had known her from the time she was fifteen. He said, 'She is never so happy as when she is miserable between love affairs' (this in reference to her much touted recent love affair with Omar Sharif). He went on, 'Somehow when one thinks of Anouk it is inevitably a tiny figure alone huddled up and sobbing in the back seat of a Rolls.'

While I photographed Anouk, she talked about her role as Justine. Justine is Jewish. Anouk, whose maiden name was Dreyfus, was born of a Jewish father and a Catholic mother. She was brought up a Catholic but had since become Jewish. Because she was immersed in her role as a Jew, she talked about it, and I'm still haunted by two things she quoted. They seemed to say more about her than anything else I experienced with her during the three weeks I knew her on the film.

Quote from Treblinka: 'The Jews are prone to anguish but seldom given to despair.'

And, said by an anonymous Jewish poet to his wife when the Nazis came to get them, 'Till now we have lived with fear, now we can know hope.'

Anouk Aimée on the set of *Justine.* Tunisia, 1968.

Audrey Hepburn interviewing a Jew who fled Morocco where there had been a frightening demonstration of anti-Semitism. This was for radio. Paris, 1968.

George C. Scott as Patton. He won an Oscar for his portrayal. Spain, 1969.

Patton

(1969)
George C. Scott
Director: Franklin J. Schaffner

(General George S. Patton Jr – 'Blood and Guts' – was a World
War II American tank commander who is mainly remembered for
his part in the Battle of the Bulge, his battles of Kasserine Pass and
El Guettar in Tunis, his sweep across Italy, France and Belgium into
the Ruhr, and the headlines he made when he slapped an American
soldier. He was relieved of his command when he was quoted as
saying, while touring German concentration camps, that the
ordinary run of Nazis aren't much different from Democrats and
Republicans back home.)

The day 20th Century-Fox killed Morgan Paul there were 2,750 for
lunch – most of them the Spanish army. A film company moves on
its belly; seventeen chefs prepared 2.4 tons of meat, ninety gallons
of coffee and baked 4,800 lunch rolls. Some 120 gallons of soft
drinks (economy size) were drunk.

The condemned man ate a hearty lunch – excellent garbanzo soup,
delicious ragout, and cheese and fruit for dessert. Morgan Paul is a
young actor who plays the part of Jensen, a lieutenant on the staff
of General Patton, who will be killed at the battle of El Guettar,
which took place in Tunis but is being photographed in Almería in
the south of Spain.

The film is being shot out of sequence. Morgan Paul, whose first
film this is, is not used to the ways of film companies. He is

confused. He picks up his tin helmet and says, 'Last week they buried me, this week they're going to kill me, and next week I do the first scene in the picture.'

During lunch, publicists have been handing out to the journalists fact sheets, production notes, actors' biographies and other data which make it easier for them to write about *Patton*. From the weight of the handouts, it seems as though more words have been written about the making of the film than there were shots fired during World War II.

One release describes *Patton* as Schaffnerian cinema. Franklin J. Schaffner (*Planet of the Apes*) is directing the movie. The interview with him quotes him as saying, 'This is a complex character, a very modern man that defies semantics.' Patton is then described variously as: bombastic, flamboyant, grandiloquent, fiery, explosive, controversial, dazzling, brilliant, vivid, flaming and 'the most winningest general in history'. The publicity goes on:

'Patton is shown as pious and profane; brutal and tender. Of some five million servicemen who went through World War II, relatively few caught a glimpse of the flamboyant, caparisoned general whose snowy guns matched his hair.'

The photographer was intrigued with the idea of the caparisoned general and his snowy guns that matched his hair, and went along to the make-up trailer where George C. Scott, who plays Patton, was having his head shaved to a bald dome.

George C. Scott is a monumentally inventive actor. It was fascinating to watch the transition of Scott to Patton. It didn't seem to be Scott, it might have been Patton, but it seemed more like 'Scotton' especially when he spoke. Patton had had a high, squeaky

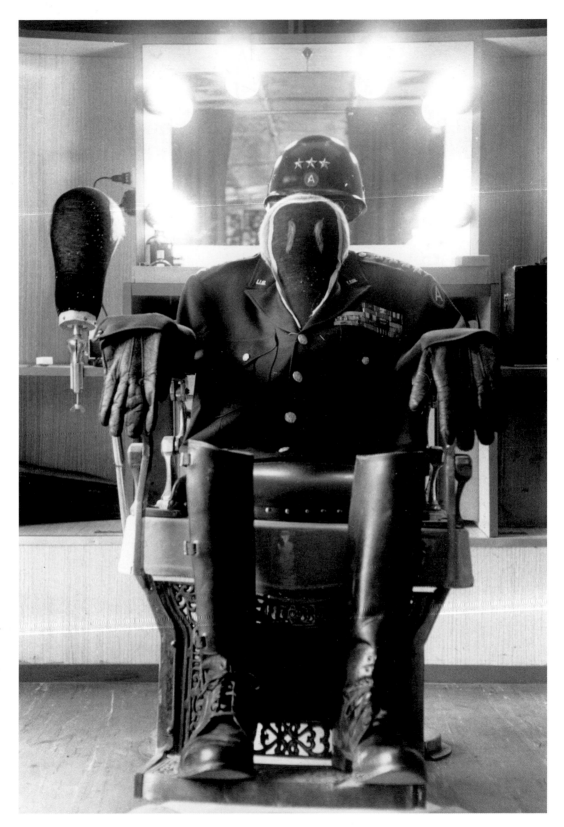

The costume (a general's outfit) is kept ready for the filming of *Patton*. Spain, 1969.

voice. My own research had dredged this up, and I kept wondering what the speeches he had made before the dash to the Ruhr would have sounded like – those profane, four-letter-word speeches in which he urged his soldiers on to battle. An earwitness told of things like, 'We'll screw their wives and daughters, and carry away as much loot as we can handle' (only he didn't say 'screw') but none of that was in the script.

While his make-up man, Del Acevedo, filled Scott's nose with mortician's wax to make it look like Patton's more patrician nose, Scott in his deep voice talked about the character: 'Actors who play themselves repeatedly bore me. That's the reason the head has been shaved, and the white wig donned, things like moles and eyebrows added and the attempt to straighten my hooked nose. Patton has a splendid, almost classic military bearing. A great cavalryman, a great rider. He believed in appearances. He was a great actor.'

While this conversation is going on, the make-up man is pasting scrim on Scott's nose to shorten it by a quarter of an inch. Then a set of dirty false teeth is introduced into Scott's mouth. The actor had noticed in a photograph that the General had had stained teeth, and had his dentist match these with both uppers and lowers that fit over his own white attractive ones.

That day in the dressing room Scott was proprietary about Patton. He felt that he was a man much misunderstood. One kept thinking, I hope he doesn't want to soften him. Of course he was a great tank commander – history please note – but he was (depending upon what one reads and hears) also a dramatic cowboy or a homicidal Boy Scout. When the wig and the eyebrows and the costume have been added, Scott *is* Patton. His concern is to make sure that

'Whatever we do, I don't want to wake up nights – and I have – thinking that General Patton is dervishing in his grave in Luxembourg over what the hell happened here. I want him to have a little respect for it.'

The make-up man backs off to inspect Scott. Finds everything OK. Twists his hand into a sloppy salute, mumbles, 'General, war is hell.'

Scott goes to rehearse a graveyard scene on the sandy desert. As he approaches the spot where two men are busily dusting out footprints with improvised sagebrush brooms and another man is dusting off wooden grave markers (both crosses and stars of David – after all, this war was being fought against the Nazis), he sees two small boys playing a war game. He stops to watch. The boys make a blasting sound – to them a gun being fired – and yell 'You're dead!' One of them hits the sands and sprawls. The dead one pops up, shoots the other, and it starts all over again.

These are Scott's two sons – Campbell, six, and Alexander, eight. Campbell is not satisfied with his death scenes, and keeps saying, 'I didn't do it right – not enough emotion.'

Scott continues to the battleground, the location where the Battle for El Guettar is being prepared. He stops to talk to the technical adviser, General Paul D. Harkins (ret. US Army), the general in Vietnam from whom Westmoreland took command in 1964. They joke about the problems involved in staging the battles. Harkins says, 'I told MacCarthy [the producer and a retired World War II brigadier general himself] I was glad I didn't have as much trouble running the real war [World War II, Korea, Vietnam]. The only resemblance it bears to real war is the confusion.'

It is hard to tell where fantasy ends and reality begins. The south of
Spain is variously Palermo, Italy; Tunisia, North Africa; and Sicily.
The Spanish army is the American army or the German army (or
both) although they are not exactly Hitler's idea of his Aryan
Wehrmacht. Not a blue eye among the 4,000 of them. The Spanish
army had been hired by Fox for the restaging and refighting of the
battles in the film.

A Spanish general is pleased with the situation because the soldiers
are learning their practice manoeuvres during the filming. It is
better than real war. Real war, you see, interferes with manoeuvres.
Yes, he explains, that's why war is hell.

Between the facts and the make-believe, the adjectives and the
hyperbole, the battle effects and the mortician's wax, the question
comes whether it is possible to make a film that will avoid creeping
John Wayneism and Hollywood heroics to tell it like it was. In a
period where we are caught between the overstatement of the anti-
hero and the Mao and Che Guevara posters of the young,
20th Century-Fox is betting $15 million that it can.

Sean Connery, Angela Allen (script lady) and Michael Caine go over script for *The Man Who Would Be King*. Morocco, 1975.

The Man Who Would Be King

(1975)
Sean Connery, Michael Caine, Christopher Plummer
Director: John Huston

I remember John Huston's dictum that when you plan a film you
must begin with a good yarn. The yarn that he talked of most often
and that seemed most elusive to him was the Kipling short story
'The Man Who Would Be King'. Huston was a prodigious reader
and had read it as a boy. He boasted that he had studied a Kipling
glossary of Anglo-Indian terms rather than algebra and that he
could quote miles of Kipling doggerel.

He had been thinking of the idea since 1952, when he and the
script writer Peter Viertel had discussed it, and the money backers
for *Moby Dick* said they would back *TMWWBK*. He was delighted to
go to India on a recce, but actually he was invited by the Maharajah
of Cooch Behar on a tiger shoot. He criss-crossed India and went to
Nepal, then Afghanistan. Somehow the film didn't come to fruition,
but in 1973 he asked Aeneas MacKenzie to do a script and Steve
Grimes, the very gifted art director, to get involved, along with
Tony Veiller.

Over the years Huston talked about the casting. He had thought the
two principals should be played by his father, Walter Huston, and
Bogart. By now they were both dead. When he spoke to Clark Gable
about it (thinking that he would pair him with Spencer Tracey)
while they were working on *The Misfits*, Gable was very
enthusiastic. Then Gable died.

The three principal actors for *The Man Who Would Be King* discuss the script:
Sean Connery, Christopher Plummer and Michael Caine. Morocco, 1975.

Huston's next choice was Paul Newman, who was to be paired with
Robert Redford. Newman was enthusiastic, too, but felt that John
should cast two Englishmen: 'John, for Christ's sake get Connery
and Caine.' Newman had cast it on the spot.

So John and his assistant Gladys Hill flew to Mexico and wrote a
script incorporating some of the best of the other existing scripts.
Then, script in hand, Huston contacted Caine, a Cockney, and
Connery, a Scotsman. They were pleased, accepted at once and in
spite of busy schedules made time – and the film was shot in 1975.
I was unable to work on the film because of prior commitments,
but was delighted to be invited for the Christmas holiday and while
in Morocco to do a few days' shooting on my own. We stayed at La
Mamounia in Marrakesh, the hotel that conjures up images of the
Arabian Nights and Scheherazade.

There are two images that I cannot forget and that I associate with
the making of the film. The first is a scene in which Connery and
Caine in tattered and unkempt uniforms march in goose-stepping
to see Christopher Plummer, who plays Kipling and is, if memory
serves, a government official. Caine reports in a Cockney accent
and Connery in Scottish – a really wonderful scene to which I later
heard a postscript from John. Sometime in the eighties he was very
ill and in hospital in California when these two rogues in hired
uniforms goose-stepped into his sickroom, speaking their lines from
the film. He was convinced he got better from that moment on.
The other image – and this one haunts me – is the picture of the
high priest. John wanted a hundred-year-old to play the part – and
found him twenty miles from Marrakesh in the Atlas Mountains.
Since he didn't speak a line, the casting director, Boatie Boatwright,

thought he would be fine and John gave him a screen test. He had never been away from his native village or been in a car, or seen a film but he came to Marrakesh, and later John got him back again to see rushes.

He sat in the dark, and when his segment came on, the tears were coursing down his cheeks. When he was asked what was the matter, he sniffed and said, 'I shall never die.'

Joe Losey, director (at Chanel's atelier), checks out the fall collections. Paris, 1977.

Irene Papas, the Greek actress who came to public attention with *Zorba the Greek*.
Just a sitting because I love her work. New York, 1978.

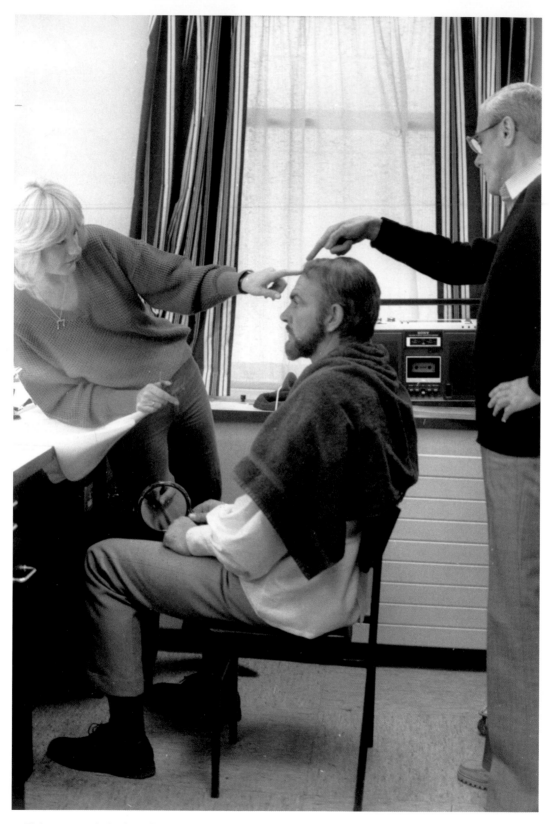

Fitting a new wig for Sean Connery's role as an elegant gentleman in *The Great Train Robbery*. Ireland, 1978.

THE GREAT TRAIN ROBBERY

(1978)
Sean Connery, Donald Sutherland
Director: Michael Crichton

'What's this then, is it a fillum?' asked the sheep farmer, who had
heard the train whistle and come running. Now he saw the ancient
train come chugging through the countryside sixty miles from
Dublin. He had seen the helicopter filming from overhead and had
heard rumours and counter-rumours, conjectures and guesses about
film stars.

After being admonished by Michael Crichton, the director, to be
quiet, he watched Sean Connery (007), in his black stovepipe hat
and his elegant black-caped coat, walk across a field and look at a
man's body with blood oozing from one ear. After the look he
walked back to a horse and carriage in which Lesley-Anne Down
(*Upstairs, Downstairs*) waited for him.

A group of locals told the farmer it was indeed a 'fillum' and gave
him some added bits of information. There had been a violent fight
in the baggage car between the dead man and the guard whose job
it was to keep the government's gold bullion from being stolen on
its way from London to Folkestone. The gold was to be shipped to
the Crimea to pay the soldiers (remember, this is 1855). Chicken
crates broke open, chicken feathers flew like snowflakes (one
chicken flew away and ran down the middle of the track – the
entire train ran over it and it remained unscathed). During the
fight, the guard kicked the man in the groin. The man in agony lost

his bearings and in trying to get away from the guard had catapulted out of the moving train.

Because they weren't aware of the common practice of making films out of sequence, the crowd had difficulty understanding that the 'dead' man was now about to leap from the train. Since it was Sean Connery who walked away from the 'dead' man and they both wore beards, the crowd mistook the stunt man for Connery.

The crowd waited patiently while three cameras were set up for the fall, Michael Crichton (film director, doctor, author of *The Great Train Robbery*, *The Andromeda Strain*, *Jurassic Park*, etc.) talked to the producer, John Foreman (*Butch Cassidy and the Sundance Kid*), while he waited for the spring clouds that covered the sun to clear long enough for the jump. It was dangerous and could be done only once. Dick Ziker (the stunt man) made the fall of fifteen feet from the moving train to the ground, hit his target, bounced and kept falling another twenty feet.

The crowd clapped and kept clapping, but the man who asked if it was a 'fillum' was especially delighted. He kept saying how wonderful it was. He thought they had thrown a dummy out of the train and couldn't imagine how they had controlled it.

This then was part of the prologue for the film – just enough to tease and excite – before we entered the world of Michael Crichton's best-seller *The Great Train Robbery*. He based it on a true story he had read, embellished it with fantasy – a mastermind (Sean Connery), a master lock-picker (Donald Sutherland), a beautiful woman (Lesley-Anne Down) who plays a lady, a bawd, a serving maid, a beggar woman – and of course the hero of the film, the enchanting chug-chug 1855 train which is totally authentic.

Working with Michael Crichton was a bonus. To see him day and night for weeks on location was a joy. To have contact with that many-layered personality was an adventure. It was stimulating to watch him think and to make decisions. We became friends and now exchange newly published books from time to time.

The Alien, who was over seven feet tall and as slim as a shoelace, with the strange body designed for him.
England, 1978.

ALIEN

(1978)
Sigourney Weaver, Tom Skerritt, John Hurt
Director: Ridley Scott
Designer: H. R. Giger

I had done my homework on H. R. Giger. On the early-morning
flight from London to see him in Zurich I checked the notes
I had made about him – really just key words to stimulate the
imagination and start the photographic juices flowing:
fantastical art/baroque images/satanic/malevolent/occult/demonic
characters/monsters/foetal figures/skulls/skeletons/cats/Black
magic/personal mythologies/nightmares/mask of death/psychogram/
Necronomicon [the name of H.R.G.'s book]/great phalluses/bio-
Mecananoid virgins/mingling of ugly and beautiful/airbrush.
Over the unappetizing aeroplane breakfast I questioned my
companion about this painter we were about to see. He was Gordon
Carroll, one of the film producers for *Alien*, who had worked on the
movie with Giger for two years. He kept putting me off. He asked
me to wait, to see for myself. I would understand when I saw Giger
in his own ambience – in his studio.
I asked about the film. It is a suspense thriller about seven
astronauts who, while working on a starship far away in space
and time, encounter an awesome galactic horror whom they try
to combat. The Alien is this horror, and Giger had designed him,
the spacecraft and parts of the mysterious planet on which he
is discovered.
Somehow my notes on Giger and the description of the film didn't

221

fit with the Giger I had met – a rather chunky middle-sized man dressed in black, who was described to me as looking like Napoleon after Waterloo. He wore a black leather coat and lots of black scarves (it had been bitterly cold on the set of the sound stage). There were contradictions here – throughout the balance of the journey I turned my mind to these. When the taxi stopped at a shabby house set in the middle of a rickety row of terraced workmen's houses in an industrial outskirt of Zurich, I thought we must be in the wrong place.

No, here was Giger greeting us at the door. Again in black, behind him Mia, his girl, also in black – leather trousers, silk shirt, black wristlets and high black heels. It was a soggy, snowy day – a day, my bones said, for light, cheerful surroundings, hot grog and open fires.

Mia said she would get us some champagne and Giger showed us around the house. On the ground floor a dining room housed a magnificent table Giger had designed (black, of course), some bentwood chairs, a sculptured automaton he had made, in the bowels of which there was a large brass platter that held some decaying apples (real), and a black cat (live). On the table there were black candles in a surreal candlestick (also Giger's handiwork). The ceiling was black; there were no windows. They had been boarded over with the huge murals that were everywhere in this tiny house. At first I was disconcerted by the murals – they had such extraordinary perspective, such depth of field, that I felt myself projected into them.

Mia came in from the kitchen with the champagne – vintage, lovely. Nice little domestic scene. She wore her apron – just like any

other housewife's, except that hers was black and had painted on
it a white skeleton. The place had human skulls everywhere, and
Giger said he owned twelve skeletons – but they were in the studio.
We went upstairs to the studio, which had a rather splendid
skylight. We were shown the skeletons. In addition to the mortal
ones, there was a lovely specimen in metal (reminded me of babies'
shoes cast in bronze, but I didn't dare ask if this was a real one
cast in metal).

Carroll and Giger settled down for two days of shooting and
talking. Giger talked about his work, which is now principally done
with airbrush. Many of the paintings, he says, are his nightmares
externalized. He loves highly stylized women, bones, skulls and
machinery. He prefers a palette of blacks, greys, beiges and browns;
when he works in colour, a single colour seems to dominate, like a
green landscape or a red woman, but actually the painting is full of
subtle tones. His influences are Cocteau, Hieronymus Bosch,
Salvador Dalí, Tantric, erotic and pop art. He collects fantastical art.

Tragedy has pursued Giger. His first passionate love, Li, killed herself
– there are rumours that she shot herself in his bedroom. In fact,
dark tales accrue to him like filings to a magnet. In London I heard
that a second girlfriend had also eliminated herself; and in New
York I was told that he keeps Li's skull in his bedroom. Certainly
there are sculptured heads and paintings of her all over the place.
In the studio there is a witch's circle where the house witch lives.
Mia giggles and says they should try to enlist her help to get the
people next door to move so they can buy the house and break
through the two to give them more room.

In order to design the Alien, Giger wanted a very very tall, very very skinny figure of a man around whom to drape black armour. After a diligent search, all seven foot eleven inches of him was found in a bar in London. He was African, thin to the point of emaciation and ebony-coloured. Perfect for Giger's needs. Giger later said of the monster he made for *Alien*, 'It is elegant, fast and terrible. It exists to destroy – and destroys to exist. Once seen, it will never be forgotten.' In the film the creature is a parasite who can reproduce himself in anyone he encounters in an outburst of blood. The creature gobbles up the space crew in the film one by one and grows enormously.

After the first day's work – between the witches and the skeletons, not to mention the black ceilings and the mind-provoking art – I was afraid that I would have nightmares. Not so. It was all so friendly and pleasant that I began to enjoy my strange surroundings, to relish pizza by candlelight and skulls, and to appreciate my gentle hosts.

There is a postscript to this story. When I went back to the London studio to do some additional shots of Giger, one of the set dressers told me that the crew loved him and that one of their members had drawn a funny picture of him in the men's toilet. While my male assistant stood guard, I went to the men's toilet with my camera. There among the four-letter graffiti I found a profile of Giger with a halo over it which read, 'Giger paints nice things in secret.'

H. R. Giger, the designer of the Alien, at his drawing board. Switzerland, 1978.

H. R. Giger, who designed the Alien, also designed the safety film sun glasses he is wearing. Switzerland, 1978.

Lord Olivier in a toga movie – but rather a good one – had difficulty remembering lines. *Clash of the Titans*.
England, 1979.

CLASH OF THE TITANS

(1979)
Laurence Olivier, Maggie Smith
Director: Desmond Davis

The call sheet listed my appointment to photograph Laurence Olivier for a *Newsweek* cover at 11 a.m. In typical Hollywood style, the stretch limo the film company had sent was on time, but Lord Olivier was not. He was struggling with his lines for *Clash of the Titans*, a toga saga being filmed outside London.

Lord Olivier hated photographers, and was known for his antipathy to them; he had told me that the night before when he was my charming dinner partner at John Schlesinger's. He went on to say they made his life a hell in the USA and spoiled his time there.

Next morning at nine when I went to shoot him at home (as had been arranged by the magazine), he was displeased, said he didn't want to be photographed at all – but then consented to go to his office nearby. The shoot there wasn't good. He then said OK, eleven o'clock at the film set.

So there I was on the film set. It was a bitch of a day. I was told no pix until four o'clock.

At the appointed time Lord Olivier was dressed, coiffed and ready for the camera – but – his lines were still a problem. However, he must have remembered our dinner conversation of the evening before, and his natural charm asserted itself. By way of apology, he mentioned that when he had been young he had learned (letter perfect) all the Henry plays in a weekend. He was gracious, consented to my shooting him as he was – toga, wig etc., legs propped on a chair and still worrying over the script lines. *Newsweek* loved the picture, they said, but decided not to run it. They decided they wanted a studio portrait instead.

Ursula Andress in *Clash of the Titans*. England, 1979.

UNDER THE VOLCANO

(1983)
Jacqueline Bisset, Albert Finney, Anthony Andrews
Director: John Huston

All the action in *Under the Volcano* takes place in agonizing flashbacks into the life of a British consul in Cuernavaca, Mexico, during an epic twenty-four-hour drunken binge on the Day of the Dead, *circa* 1938. There are strange and visually provocative scenes in the film – for instance, the celebration of the Day of the Dead, when relatives of the deceased bring their food and drink to the cemetery and picnic at the graveside. And a scene with eighteen prostitutes, a dwarf and a transvestite – all of them local talent who had been hired from the local whorehouses. To say nothing of the terrifying death scenes of the consul and his wife.

Malcolm Lowry's book was wonderfully graphic but sprawling and difficult to translate to film. For years John Huston had tried various writers, but there never seemed to be a workable script until a young producer, Michael Fitzgerald, had Guy Gallo, a scriptwriter only twenty-eight years old, take a crack at it.

Screenplay:

Guy Gallo as a student saw in the *New York Times* a list of twenty-five writers asked to name their favourite book and lo, *Under the Volcano* was on practically every writer's list. He got the book, and during his first year at Yale Drama School an independent producer suggested he write a film treatment. Gallo wrote a film script in

John Huston directing *Under the Volcano*. The death masks are for celebration of the Day of the Dead. Cuernavaca, Mexico, 1983.

seven days, only to discover that the man didn't own the rights and had also lost interest in the project.

Three years later, in April 1982, Michael Fitzgerald, as John Huston's producer, asked Annette Insdorf of the *New York Times* for a young writer who might work on *The Rack*. When he was contacted, Guy said he could send along his work on *Under the Volcano* as a sample of what he could do. Fitzgerald was not much interested but told Huston about *Under the Volcano*. Huston was very much interested and assigned the script to Guy.

When Gallo started on the script, he was daunted by the book. Then in his research he read a letter from Lowry to Frank Taylor, his editor, about a script he (Lowry) and his wife Marjorie had done for Hollywood on *Tender Is the Night*, in which he said, 'We've left out enough for a Puccini opera, but here it is.' This gave Guy the courage to write his Lowry script.

The Production:

Interviewed Tom Shaw, the second-unit head. The reason it moves at breakneck speed in the shooting, he told me, is that Huston knows exactly what cuts together with what. He doesn't dither and do the usual close, medium and long shot as well as over-the-shoulder shots that less experienced directors do for each situation – it's usually one or at most two shots. When he gets what he needs and wants, he stops.

Besides, Finney's certainty and professionalism are so great and his timing so fine that he usually gets everything in one take. And then there's the use of the Steadicam, which saves endless time laying track and re-lighting the scene. This way of working – the fast-moving, flowing Panaglide shots and the decisive action of director and star – makes the use of 'time' an integral part of the film (all action takes place in twenty-four hours) and provides the necessary unity essential to making the picture believable. It also raises the level for everyone around them. John Huston says that if you work with a 'company' producer, if you're one day behind, he figures you're $40,000 over budget, but if you're one day ahead, he figures you're $4,000 ahead.

The Extras:
The Mexican townspeople are wonderfully sweet, agreeable and giving – they are patient, do whatever they are asked to do and earn the equivalent of six dollars a day. The gringos are touchy, slightly disillusioned – each one expects to be 'discovered' in this film – never satisfied, picky. They complain mildly – Can I bring my aunt? I don't like this dress (or wig or whatever) – and although on the day of the ballroom scene they were given an excellent lunch, there was still fault-finding. They earn twenty dollars a day.

Bullfight Scenes:
The script required Anthony Andrews to fight a bull. He gets drunk, drops from the terrace into the bullring where he is drinking with his half-brother, the consul (whose wife has been his lover), and fights and kills a bull. Since Andrews had no idea how to proceed, a young toreador was engaged to teach him a few passes. So involved did he become in the project that he not only did his own passes, but the day after the film bull had been killed by the real torero, Anthony did fight a bull, but did it for his own satisfaction and refused to have it photographed.

The local whores from Mexico City were recruited in John Huston's film *Under the Volcano*. All of these women had a ball being in the film. Cuernavaca, Mexico, 1983.

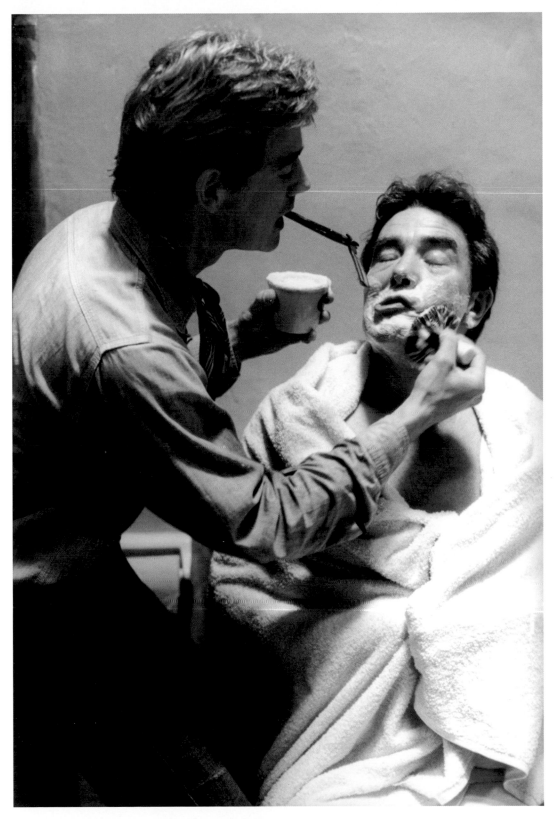

Anthony Andrews shaves a drunken Albert Finney who is celebrating the Day of the Dead.
Under the Volcano. Cuernavaca, Mexico, 1983.

WHITE NIGHTS

(1984)

Mikhail Baryshnikov, Isabella Rossellini, Gregory Hines,
Helen Mirren, Geraldine Page
Director: Taylor Hackford

'Not too glam!' the director called to the actress, who stood
silhouetted by the light coming off the sound stage. The three
professionals who surrounded her to check wardrobe, hair and
make-up nodded. It was a familiar refrain, one they heard daily.
It was their job to make Isabella Rossellini, one of the world's
highest-paid models, into a Russian character. Except for a light
dusting of powder to keep off the shine and a touch of lip rouge for
colour, there was no make-up. For further authenticity, her clothes
were a wardrobe mistress's idea of what a Soviet woman in Moscow
would wear: a dirndl skirt with horizontal stripes, a cheap cotton
shirt, socks and sandals. It had been agreed from the beginning
that glamour would be submerged to let the actress emerge.
Now Taylor Hackford, the director, came over to check before
Isabella went before his cameras for the first time. He had done a
great deal of planning with her. At the preproduction stage there
had been lengthy discussions about her role, and before preliminary
rehearsals he had sent her to Russia with Gregory Hines (who plays
her husband on screen) to get a sense of the life of the country and
the people, to listen to their voices and to develop a rapport
with Greg.
It was obvious that the idea had worked: there was an easy
camaraderie between them. Their weeks of rehearsals with the third

Misha Baryshnikov at rehearsal for the American Ballet Theatre during filming of *White Nights*.
New York, 1984.

lead, Mikhail Baryshnikov, had also forged a friendship among the three of them. To me watching them, it seemed that they were drawn close together by their common situation. Although each had worked in front of a camera before, their careers were peripheral to motion pictures. None had been a full-time actor, each had been pre-eminent in his (or her) chosen field: Baryshnikov in ballet, Hines in tap dancing and musicals, and Rossellini as a TV reporter and comedienne in Italy and as an international model. (In addition, she had the burden of having a great deal expected of her because she is Ingrid Bergman and Roberto Rossellini's daughter.) Now they were all taking calculated risks in branching out.

Never before having had lead roles in a major international Hollywood movie, they were to carry the responsibility for a film which cost millions.

It was these elements of chance, this Russian roulette, so to speak, that intrigued me. The photographer is really a gambler. Every component she works with is variable, from the camera equipment she chooses to the emulsion on the film, the light source and the expression on the subject's face. They are endlessly changeable and interchangeable, and the choices (and results) are myriad. In photographing stills on a film, the practitioner has an additional ingredient to cope with. On set the light is dictated by the lighting cameraman, further narrowing the photographer's sense of control. Also, tensions on a film set are generally high. Time is of the essence, because costs must be of paramount consideration and deadlines must be met. There is little or no extra time for anything except keeping the film quality at peak and getting it done on schedule. Anything that interferes with this is usually given short shrift, and the outside photographer coming in has to be on the qui vive and be prepared to make do, to improvise, to look out for every chance opportunity for the unusual picture.

I had been assigned by European and American magazines to do a picture essay on Isabella, so she became the main focus of my interest. I had seen countless smooth retouched pictures of her as the Lancôme model, neck draped in silks or sables, in the glossy magazines. Usually she was served up as a glorious disembodied head (the image the photographers call the 'John the Baptist shot'.) She was not only in the advertisements, but on countless covers. The image was of great aloof elegance, but even though all lines were removed, what came through was a woman, not a commodity which had resulted from the light and shadow of the portraitist and the pencil of the retoucher.

She was open, warm, funny, with a great bubbling laugh, and she had an acute mind. Shy at first and then forthcoming with observations, anecdotes and laughter. She had her mother's mouth and her father's personality. She took her work seriously, but not herself seriously. Over the time we saw each other during and after the filming, what came through was Swedish reserve and Italian ebullience.

She would tell jokes on herself and send herself up. She talked about the problem of replacing her Italian accent with a Russian accent. She worked diligently with Seva, her Russian coach, on her speech, and when she felt secure in her delivery, she called friends in Italy to dazzle them with her Russian accent. But – and here amusement burst forth, choking her with giggles – she said her friends thought it was the Pope speaking.

The director Taylor Hackford and part of his cast (including Isabella Rossellini) and crew of *White Nights* check out a shot they have just made on the monitor. Finland, 1984.

The working days with Isabella (on the sound stage in England and on location in Finland and Portugal) were harmonious until we got to the love scenes. Then both she and Gregory, her on-screen husband, were suddenly diffident and reluctant about still pictures. It was not surprising. It's a daunting prospect to take off your clothes and go to bed with a colleague in the glare of klieg lights and the wide-screen probing camera eye in front of a crew of strangers. And that is only the beginning – the actors are then expected to create an illusion of tenderness and intimacy that will be utterly believable to the viewer.

It was a first for both actors, and it presented emotional problems, technical problems and time problems: emotional problems because it was an extremely demanding scene; technical problems because it was to be shot by remote control from outside the tiny bedroom with no one inside but the actors and the director; and time problems because Taylor Hackford wanted spontaneity, which meant avoiding doing scenes over and over again. The actors and director had to be in sync about the way the action would be played between this disparate pair – he an American black and she a Catholic Italian.

The presence of the stills photographer created an additional problem to the already fraught situation. Actors are not happy at being identified with this kind of picture, which has a way of appearing years later to embarrass them. In context on film it is part of the whole, to round out the character. As a photo by itself, it depends upon the way it is used and the way it is captioned. If used badly and captioned unscrupulously, at best it can misrepresent and at worst it can be damaging. Then there were the physical problems

– there was no room in the small bedroom and my presence might interfere with the actors' concentration.

We had built up mutual trust over the time we had worked together, both at work and off the set, and we arrived at a possible solution. I would be able to shoot during briefing, preparation and rehearsal, then leave, watch the scene being filmed on the video monitor, then run back in for a few minutes – before lights were shifted for the next take – to get the stills. My responsibility was to work at speed so as not to interfere with either the work of the crew or the mood of the actors who would be replaying their love scenes for my camera. Since the scene was intended as a gentle and loving one between man and wife, I tried to keep it that way by showing in the expressions on their faces (and the upper part of the body) their affection, concern and appreciation of each for the other.

And of course David Watkin, the lighting cameraman, whose low-key dramatic lighting was perfect for the film, gave the stills people nightmares. It was wonderful to see the dancers (on screen) move in and out of the light, but for stills it created problems that we had to be ingenious enough either to use or to overcome. The cine film, which is projected, has the advantage of having light shine through transparent material so that low-key lighting has a luminosity about it, but the still photograph is printed on opaque paper and the dark quality in colour has a tendency to go muddy. For black-and-white stills it can be very dramatic.

From the shoot and the film itself, bright impressions remain: Isabella's laughter, Greg's taps, Misha's intensity and passion in his acting and his dance, Taylor's utter professionalism.

Isabella Rossellini studying lines for *Blue Velvet*. Massachusetts, 1984.

Misha and Tim the dog play a game. Tim is a mongrel that Misha found. New York, 1984.

Eve Arnold by Henri Cartier-Bresson. London, 1998.

BIOGRAPHY

Eve Arnold was born in Philadelphia, Pennsylvania, of immigrant Russian parents. She began photographing while working at a photo-finishing plant in New York City in 1946, then studied photography (for six weeks) with Alexei Brodovitch at New York City's New School for Social Research in 1948. She became a full member of Magnum Photos in 1955 after being associated with it since 1951. Based in America through the fifties, Eve Arnold moved to England in 1962 and has lived there since apart from a six-year hiatus (working in China and America to prepare books on those countries).

Arnold had her first major solo exhibition in 1980 at the Brooklyn Museum. That same year, she received the National Book Award for her book *In China* and was awarded the Lifetime Achievement Award from the American Society of Magazine Photographers. In 1995 she was made a Fellow of the Royal Photographic Society and also elected 'Master Photographer', the world's most prestigious photographic honor, awarded by New York's International Center of Photography. In 1996 she was the recipient of the Kraszna-Krausz Book Award for her book *In Retrospect* and in July 2001 was made Doctor of the Arts by the Royal Academy of Arts. Eve Arnold has also been awarded honorary degrees from universities including The University of St Andrews, Scotland, and Staffordshire University.

Eve Arnold's major publications include: *The Unretouched Woman* (1976), *Flashback! The 1950s* (1978), *In China* (1980), *In America* (1983), *Marilyn Monroe, An Appreciation* (1987), *Private View: Mikhail Baryshnikov's American Ballet Theatre* (1988), *All in a Day's Work* (1989), *Eve Arnold: In Britain* (1996), *In Retrospect* (1996), *Women to Women* (1999) and *Magna Brava – Magnum's Women Photographers* (1999).

She has had innumerable exhibitions of her work principally in: the National Portrait Gallery and the Barbican in London, the Scottish National Portrait Gallery, the Gallery of Photography, Dublin, the Ikon Gallery, Birmingham, in Britain and the International Center of Photography, New York, and the Menil Museum, Houston, in America.

INDEX OF PHOTOGRAPHS

WITH THANKS TO

Bob Gottlieb for all he taught me.

Lin Campbell for her manifold abilities which she has used on my behalf.

My son Frank who was a decisive help when I felt like giving up.

My sister Gertrude who came to London when I needed her —
and helped more than she will ever know.

Carmen Pombo who looked after me and kept my small household running.

Eva Monley, Andrea Tana and Jill Robinson who knew Hollywood
and provided information.

Ruth Vitale who sent flowers and Corinne Laurie who sent chicken soup.

Ed Victor who counselled me wisely.

The Magnum Photos people who were involved in the project: to the Paris Magnum
staff and Agnes Sire for her editorial skill with photographs; to Liz Grogan and her
London staff for the printing, digitizing and other necessary hard work that
goes with preparing a book for layout.

Glen Brent, my wonderful printer, who met deadlines without complaint.

Barney Wan for invaluable advice about layout and production.

My dear friend Hanan Al-Shaykh who was a listening ear in times of stress.

Claudine Paquot, my editor at Cahiers du Cinema, who cheerfully made trips from
Paris to London to work on the book and managed to laugh at our various cultural
differences and misunderstandings.

All of you and the numerous others who helped beyond the call of friendship.
I salute you and thank you. Without you my *Film Journal* could not
have been published.